Amrit Wilson was born in Calcutta in 1941 and lived in various towns and cities of Bengal and Northern India until 1961, when she came to Britain as a student. Originally a research chemist, she became a freelance journalist in 1974, writing mainly about racism, the experiences of black workers in Britain, and women's rights. In particular she has been concerned with Asian women in Britain, and her articles have appeared in the *Guardian, The Times Educational Supplement, New Society* and *Spare Rib*. She speaks Hindi, Urdu and Bengali, and has been working on this book for several years, talking to Asian women about the problems they face inside and outside their communities, their feelings about the two cultures which are part of their daily lives, and their prospects for the future. Amrit Wilson lives in London, and is at present editor of *Poverty and Power*, the magazine published by War on Want. She is married and has a twelve-year-old daughter.

VIRAGO
is a feminist publishing company:

'It is only when women start to organise
in large numbers that we become a
political force, and begin to move towards
the possibility of a truly democratic society
in which every human being can be brave,
responsible, thinking and diligent in the struggle
to live at once freely and unselfishly'

SHEILA ROWBOTHAM
Women, Resistance and Revolution

VIRAGO
Advisory Group

Andrea Adam	Jane Gregory
Carol Adams	Christine Jackson
Sally Alexander	Suzanne Lowry
Anita Bennett	Jean McCrindle
Liz Calder	Nancy Meiselas (*U.S.A.*)
Bea Campbell	Mandy Merck
Angela Carter	Cathy Porter
Mary Chamberlain	Elaine Showalter (*U.S.A.*)
Deirdre Clark	Spare Rib Collective
Anna Coote	Mary Stott
Jane Cousins	Anne Summers (*Australia*)
Bobbie Crosby	Rosalie Swedlin
Nicci Crowther	Michelene Wandor
Anna Davin	Alison Weir
Rosalind Delmar	Elizabeth Wilson
Zoe Fairbairns	Women and Education
Carolyn Faulder	Barbara Wynn

Finding a Voice

ASIAN WOMEN IN BRITAIN

Amrit Wilson

Virago
London

to my mother and my father

Published by VIRAGO Limited 1978
5 Wardour Street, London W1V 3HE

Reprinted 1979

Copyright © Amrit Wilson 1978

ISBN 0 86068 011 8 Casebound Edition
ISBN 0 86068 012 6 Paperback Edition

Typeset by Preface Limited, Salisbury, Wilts
Printed in Great Britain by litho
at The Anchor Press, Tiptree, Essex

Contents

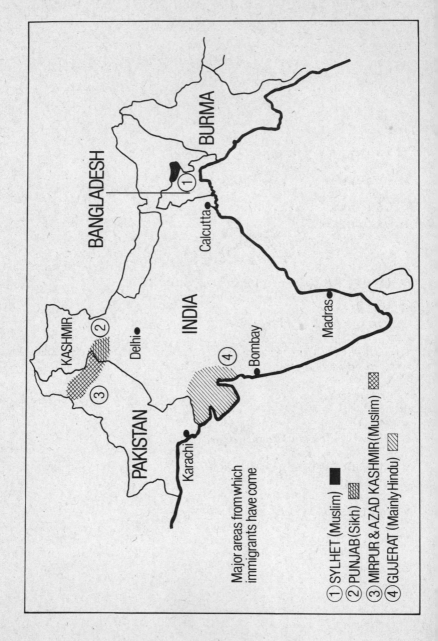

Major areas from which immigrants have come

① SYLHET (Muslim) ■
② PUNJAB (Sikh) ▦
③ MIRPUR & AZAD KASHMIR (Muslim) ▨
④ GUJERAT (Mainly Hindu) ▨

INDIA

Rural areas of Punjab and Gujerat and a much smaller number of people from cities

PAKISTAN

Rural areas of Punjab and Azad Kashmir and a much smaller number of people from cities

BANGLADESH

Villages of Sylhet district and a smaller number of people from cities

Immigration chiefly in first half of this century. More Gujeratis emigrated than Punjabis

Immigration chiefly in first half of this century.

EAST AFRICA

From Kenya c. 1968

From Tanzania c. 1970

From Uganda c. 1972

From Malawi c. 1975

Men emigrated in 50s, women began to join husbands in 60s

Men emigrated mainly in 50s, women began to join husbands in late 60s and 70s

Men emigrated mainly in 50s, women began to join husbands in 70s

BRITAIN

BRITAIN

Table 1: patterns of emigration from Asia. See also Tables 2 and 3 on pages 176 and 177.

Acknowledgements

Perhaps it is always difficult to write acknowledgements but with this book it is particularly so. Most of the women who helped me did so at their own risk and their names must not be mentioned. Without their strength and inspiration and their constantly urging me on I would never have been able to write this book. I would like to thank them too for making me realise that in trying to describe their lives and identities I was also seeking to understand my own.

Of the people whose names I can mention I would like especially to thank Geeta Amin, Afshan Begum, Hashmat Ara Begum, Fatma Dharamsi, Hermione Harris, A. Sivanandan, Gina Skelton, for their enthusiasm, support and criticism.

The Prisoner

This poem was written in Bengali in 1960. It was translated into English by the author for inclusion in this book.

Shut up tight in a cheap tin trunk
hidden under a mountain of musty mattresses and torn quilts
cast away in the kitchen's sooty corner, it moans – the prisoner.
Its colour – still purple like the waves when the sea is angry
its border – still liquid gold like the sun in summer
its every fold still holds millions of petals, russet, which the
    autumn showers while passing.
'Take me out, take me out, wear me,' it cries
but none hears it cry, no one cares –
for she whose it was lies dying, giving birth to her ninth – with luck
    a son maybe.

suddenly a miracle happens someone is stirred to her depth.

In one of her countless flittings
from the kitchen to the bedroom and then on to the lean-to
– where death is vying with birth –
she, the sixteen year old, puzzled weary dishevelled, pauses for
    breath
rests her tired head on the torn quilt   .
– when the miracle happens
The voice, soft yet persistent goes on pleading, 'take me out, take
    me out try me on . . .
my angry purple will go so well with your burnished brown,
my sunlit border flashes like lightning on your monsoon cloud
    hair
my russet petals will gather up your lissom body to their hearts of
    flower
try me on once – on you, sixteen – you are sixteen only once –
    remember?'

Her eyes begin to shine, her mind wanders with desire
her body is a flute quivering for the petal strokes of the wondrous
    lover.

'Where is my rice?' shouts the father, 'everyday, must it be late?' he
    mutters

A miserable lowly, ill-paid clerk, shrivelled up untimely
with endless worries of making two ends meet.
'Water, a little warm water,' wails the dying woman in her lean-to.
'We are hungry,' shrieks the battalion of young sisters and
    brothers.

Waking up with a jolt, ashamed, repentant, the sixteen-year-old
bends down to scold the allurer; 'look what you've done! Not
    now,
not now, not now, this is not the time, later may be – not now –
    can't you hear the cries'.
'I can', says the sari sighing, 'I can – she too said the same –
'some other time' – she who is lying in the lean-to, dying; the time
    never came to her'.

Days pass – months – sixteen turns seventeen; tongues wag,
    neighbours sleepless
most keen to know what's been happening, what's wrong –
for 'Our Leela was married and a mother of two at her age'.
So to set the wrong right the wretched father pulls his belt tight
and sells his house outright – 'What else can I do?' he asks
and finds no answer – for *all* know a daughter means disaster.
With the dowry money merrily jingling, the oily priest mantras
    mumbling
with the deafening blowing of conch shells and burning of incense
with the lavish pouring of melted butter, the holy fire benignly
    glowing
– the marriage is solemnised.
At an auspicious hour of a starlit night
the father gives the daughter away to a man he does not know
    quite
knotted to a stranger – the husband to be – just behind him seven
seven times round the fire, modestly careful, seven small steps
    takes she
bowing her veiled head, she accepts her destiny and becomes his
    wife
and enters new life.

In the father-in-law's house under the eye of the mother-in-law
    queen,
in the maddening jungle of inquisitive in-laws – sisters, brothers,
    cousins, easily umpteen –

days pass, become months, then years – round the clock
cook food, serve guests, wash plates, tend the old, nurse the sick
on the move from the kitchen to the bedroom to the lean-to
the flood is on, sons come, follow daughters –
some die, some remain
a little joy, more pain –
two slave chained together, whipped by life
no time to sit together, chat together, laugh together, know each
    other
– no time to shed tears –
Why does the spring come, the cuckoo call and the trees sing
– Who hears?

'You fool, the cuckoo calls for you to hear', says the sari
'the trees sing for you to laugh, not to fear' says the sari
'the spring has come to fill your heart' says the sari
'You fool, I am here for you to wear' says the sari
'have me on', pleads the sari
'my angry purple grown soft with age will hide your pallor well,
my border, now like the sun when the day is dying, will hide those
    streaks of grey
my russet petals yellow tinged with approach of winter will sigh
    for that lissom body
– but sighing will embrace you – with grace
take me out, wear me once, time is passing,' sobs the sari.

Sighing the busy housewife says 'I know what you say is true
yet I must rush, have to go, get ready, have a lot to do
My mother-in-law's great Guru will be here in an hour or two
and with him will come his disciples, at least fifty-two.
So – not now, not now, some other time, later maybe, you see
I must fly, time is passing'.
'I can see' sobs the sari 'time is passing'.

Days have passed become months become years
Alone in the darkening shadows sits she musing
– life is nothing only tears –
'You are right,' whispers the sari, all in tatters
– 'Life is nothing only tears.'

                                        Amiya Rao

Introduction

'Women hold up half the sky'

'People come to a new country, they start a new life; but the past they can't forget it. They bring it with them –memories, attitudes and relationships.' That is what Shahida, a woman from Lahore, told me. To give a full picture of this past is a daunting task, not within the scope of this book. But the attitudes and relationships which haunt the present – what are they and how did they dominate in the past? And which past?

The women in this book fall essentially into two groups – those who come directly from certain peasant societies of India, Pakistan and Bangladesh and those whose families migrated from the same peasant backgrounds first to East Africa and then to Britain. Women of the first group are in many ways utterly dissimilar from each other, differing in language, religion and customs (see tables 1 and 2), but their roles in the peasant societies they have come from have a lot in common. It is these roles and how they were established that I shall describe in this chapter.

The Pakistani village of Mohinuddinpur was described to me by Shamim, a woman who now lives in Bradford.

Our whole village is made up of our *Biradiri* (brethren). All the people there are our brothers and sisters and relations so there are very few strangers around and women don't have to wear *Burkhas*. Anyway, *Burkha* or no *Burkha*, one has to work, cutting the fodder, cleaning out the cowsheds, working in the fields at harvest time and then cooking and cleaning – and so many other tasks.

Shamim's village is like many others from which Pakistani immigrants have come to Britain. They represent a peasant society, not, as the cliché has it, impenetrable or unchanging, but one extremely sensitive to internal change and outside influences, one where economic survival determines life styles and attitudes. Beneath the details of everyday life which Shamin describes is a feudal economy where small farmers scratch out a living from day to day, where one false step can mean falling into debt or mortgaging one's land without hope of recovery and where one rebellious individual can place the entire economic unit, the joint family, at risk. The economy of these villages – in Mirpur, Jhelum or in East Punjab across the Indo-Pakistan border (see Table 1 & map) – has been feudal for centuries. But it is a feudalism where inequalities and poverty have been intensified by British colonialism and which has in the last thirty years (since independence) been in a state of flux caused by the varying stages of capitalism which reach out to it from the towns and cities of the Indian subcontinent. But colonialism, the tensions caused by a feudal economy's reaction to capitalism and finally the effects of capitalism itself have all been imposed on a social structure which can be traced much further back. It is a structure essentially tribal in Pakistan, caste-based in India, which, though distorted several times over by a changing economy, still retains some of its concepts (including that of the position of women) in their original form. The role of women is determined by this earlier social structure and the economic influences it faces.

How did successive economic regimes affect for instance, the lives of people in the villages of India? In the province of Punjab the most important economic change of the nineteenth century came with British colonialism. Before Punjab came under British rule in 1849 the peasants had had a right to farm the land but had not owned it, in the sense of being able to sell it off. The British established individual property rights and, with these rights, a new cash tax called land revenue. The peasants who cultivated the land became its owners and proprietors and a new law of inheritance was established by which when a man died his land was equally divided among his sons. The land revenue tax (at first as much as a third of a peasant's gross yearly produce) had to be paid no matter how bad the harvest or how impoverished the family became as a result. In addition the fact that it had to be paid in cash meant that the farmers had to sell their crop to the grain-dealer and then often enough borrow money from the money lender. In East Punjab these were usually the same man, almost invariably a Brahmin by caste. In this way the British created the situation of the small farmer, destroyed him by taxation, and raised on his back a new exploiting class, the money lenders. Because the money lenders were usually Brahmins, the effect of colonialism was to strengthen the caste system and place it firmly on a class basis.

The farms, small to start with and made even smaller as time went on by the system of inheritance, were extremely vulnerable to natural disaster. One small drought would be enough to drive a farming family into debt. Often enough the farmer ended up an owner-tenant with his land mortgaged to the money lender. After that there was little point in investing money or effort into the land because there was no chance of financial recovery. In this life of stress there was only one source of hope – having sons. A family with many sons could farm its land successfully without the burden of paying farm workers and could if necessary send a son to work in the nearest town or city to earn money to pay back debts or to buy more land. Without sons there was no hope of survival. Why sons and not daughters? Because the social structure in the villages was one based on patriarchal families, where the daughter is invariably given away in marriage, and where, because a woman's chief economic role is as a producer of labour power (her sons) she is not considered of any real economic value before she is married.

This system, with its total sexual division of work, is mirrored (not caused) by the religious prescriptions for male and female roles. In both Islam and Hinduism the woman's role is domestic and decreed to be so. (For example Manu the lawgiver recommended to Hindu society more than twelve centuries ago that 'the chief function of a woman is to give birth, nurse those who are born and attend daily duties': or 'A girl must be married before she attains puberty and after she is married she must be kept busy looking after elders, cooking, cleaning, keeping accounts and saving money and of course doing *Dharma*.') Naturally these rules were and still are interpreted for the economic convenience of society. In general the work in the fields is done by men; women usually harvest only lighter crops, tend the animals and do the fatiguing work of cooking and carrying food to the fields for their men (in other words servicing labour). But more than anything else women produce the labour force – sons.

A man's role is thus within his control. He has to work hard in the fields. He may fail as a result of natural disasters but no one can blame him for that. But a woman's success or otherwise is not within her control. It is a matter of chance. She might not be able to produce the required number of sons or she might produce only daughters or she might even be childless. She is encouraged by religion, mythology and custom to produce sons. A new daughter-in-law is greeted by her mother-in-law with the blessing 'may you have seven sons' or urged formally to 'bathe in milk and you'll have lots of sons'.

But what if she fails? Society responds with oppression, which it justifies by again invoking myths, scriptures (quoted or misquoted) and proverbs, some ancient and some only a few years old, thrown up by the needs of everyday life. A woman with many daughters and no sons is considered not only unfortunate but a carrier of misfortune. A woman with no children may well be regarded as a witch who must be ostracised and barred from celebrations. As a result women themselves might well come to believe (incorrectly) that 'it is written in the *Guru Nanak's Granth Sahib* (the holy book of the Sikhs) that if you have bad *Karma* you have more girls than boys'.

The most important and uncontrollable factor in this peasant society occurs then in a woman's body. The result is that religion and superstition centre their attention on the womb in an effort to explain away in terms of 'morality' what remains unexplained and unacceptable in terms of fact. Morality and religion open the door to oppression but in focusing so sharply on the woman's role they make her the central symbol of the culture. She is the link between economic survival and the meaning of life, between economic security and emotional security. Her role is at the heart, the core of the civilisation. That is why she is kept in her place, if necessary by the most brutal oppression. If she rebels, the society itself may be overthrown.

This impossible linking role, this almost schizophrenic position which a woman has to defend is reflected over and over again at different times and in many aspects of her life. Her birth is almost invariably a disappointment to her family (because it is not a son who has been born). But soon these feelings change to love and affection. She often becomes very close to her parents, particularly her mother. However, when she gets married and goes to live in her parents-in-law's home, her father and mother hardly ever visit her. If a Muslim, she usually marries a cousin who lives in the same village so at least the surroundings are familiar to her; but among Hindus and Sikhs the husband's family nearly always live in a different village (because a woman must marry outside her kin). The bride's parents are by tradition not permitted to accept the hospitality of her in-laws. In parts of Punjab they must not spend even a single night in their village. A Sikh woman from Jullunder, recently arrived in Britain, described what her feelings had been when her daughter got married six years ago. 'Yes, I wished I could see her. I felt so sad but if I had gone there and seen her, how would I have felt? At home she was a queen, I never liked her to do the heavy jobs. There she is a slave. I know, because my life was the same. But to see her like that would hurt my feelings and hurt our *Izzat* (pride).'

This *Izzat* can also be translated as honour, self-respect and sometimes plain male ego. It is a quality basic to the emotional life of Punjab. It is essentially male but it is women's lives and actions which affect it most. A woman can have *Izzat* but it is not her own – it is her husband's or father's. Her *Izzat* is a reflection of the male pride of the family as a whole. Farda, a girl from Jhelum, told me:

If a man has a daughter she must be properly dressed, married at a reasonable age, taught to behave modestly in the presence of strangers. All these things are related to the Izzat of the girl – saving her Izzat (and through that their own Izzat) is perhaps the greatest responsibility of her parents or guardian. Because people don't want this responsibility they prefer having sons.

The joint or extended family is the peasant economic unit essential for survival. Izzat serves as its identity and gives it continuity and 'worth'. Since the same concept occurs in an even stronger form among groups like the Pathans who still retain their tribal structure, it is possible that this particular form of family identity originated in the strife- and tension-ridden relationships between Muslim tribes. It remains overshadowed by tension and the fear of violence and humiliation. (It is in this sense a quality which is likely to be inflamed in the racism of British society.) When a girl gets married her parents are traditionally considered to be in a humiliating position vis à vis her parents-in-law. They forfeit the right to stand up against them. It is thus recognised that in her parents-in-law's home a girl is completely vulnerable and any resentment against her parents may be taken out on her. As time passes the new bride is expected to take on the identity of her new family, making her subjugation complete. A woman belongs to the men in her own family, then to the men in her husband's family, but never, never to herself. A Punjabi Hindu wedding song sung by women while the bride and groom walk seven times round the wedding fire expresses this quite clearly:

Here she takes the first round,
Her grandfather's granddaughter.
Here she takes the second round,
Her maternal uncle's maternal niece.
Here she takes the third round,
Her father's elder brother's daughter.
Here she takes the fourth round
Her father's own daughter.
Here she takes the fifth round
Her father's younger brother's niece.
Here she takes the sixth round,
Her brother's sister.
Here she takes the seventh round
And lo! the darling becomes alien.

(From Oscar Lewis: *Village Life in Northern India*, Random House, New York, 1958)

In peasant societies outside Punjab – in Gujerat or Bangladesh – Izzat does not exist in quite the same form but the role of the woman remains almost identical. There too her parents who love her so much and suffer so much when she leaves their family feel indebted to her parents-in-law. There too she is never considered a significant contributor to the economic needs of the family (because labour power is not equated with real economic value) and there too, among the farming castes, her most important economic roles are the production and servicing of labour.

If the Hindus and Sikhs of Punjab have taken over the concept of Izzat from the Muslims, the Muslims and Sikhs have adopted the dowry system from the Hindus. In India, dowry taking has long been forbidden by law but it persists strongly even in the cities. In the villages the amounts given as a dowry vary from area to area and community to community, but within any community they depend on the status of the bridegroom and his family. The relationship between the size of a dowry and status makes the dowry system easily adaptable to a class society, which means that as the economies of the villages move unevenly towards capitalism the dowry system remains of vital significance both as an essential accompaniment to and a reflection of this change. For parents, the dowry system is yet another reason why having daughters may mean financial ruin.

The dowry system has sometimes been considered as an effect of the sexual division of labour where, although women do some of the heaviest work (servicing labour and producing it), these roles are considered less important than those of men. Another obvious effect of this segregation of roles is the existence of sexual hierarchies within the community. 'Men have authority over women because *Allah* has made one superior to the other, and because they spend their wealth to maintain them' says the *Koran*. But in Indian and Pakistani joint families, things are not so simple. There is a rigid hierarchy but it is not just a sexual hierarchy. A woman does, as she gets older, achieve a certain status in the joint family, particularly if she has had sons. Younger men must show their respect for her and obey her. She can treat younger women or women without status (like her husband's widowed sisters) as she likes. When finally she becomes a mother-in-law she is entitled to tyrannise her daughter-in-law, reminding her that 'I have suffered in my time now it is your turn'. To serve and suffer is considered not only a woman's lot but *right*. If a woman is suffering things are as they should be.

But even in the most oppressive family and community women do have one consolation – each other's company and affection. The warmth which sisters and sisters-in-law may show for one another can cushion a woman against the harshness of her life. The importance of this love and its physical demonstration is acknowledged in ceremonies and rituals all over the Indian sub-continent. In Muslim families, for example, it is the women in the family who are the chief mourners if someone dies. They are the ones, too, who celebrate a birth. In each case women from neighbouring and related families come to mourn or rejoice with them. The support they give may sometimes be formal, but it is never sterile or mechanical (as it often is in industrial societies). For example, when the forty days of mourning a death are over and the women in the family who have foregone food or combing their hair can start a normal life again, it is their female friends and sisters who cook for them and comb and oil their hair.

These relationships, and the position of the woman as symbolic of her culture, are mutually reinforcing. But the role of the woman, both cultural and economic, is constantly being shaped and shifted by economic and structural forces – those of colonialism and capitalism for example. It is possible to understand this by looking in some detail at a specific village. Such studies are rare, but luckily one exists of an area from which emigration to Britain has occurred (Mamdani: *The Myth of Population Control*, Monthly Review Press, 1972).

The village is Manupur in the Ludhiana district of East Punjab. The life of the farming families here has been harsh for hundreds of years but this harshness has been intensified by the laws on land inheritance and land revenue introduced by the British, which have already been described. By the 1920s Manupur, like so many other villages in Punjab, was dominated by the moneylending class who were Brahmins by caste. After World War I, 50 per cent of the land was mortgaged to moneylenders by owner-tenant farmers. These farmers had no money for improving agricultural methods and no motivation either because they realised that 'however beneficial any methods of agricultural technology were in the abstract, the benefits reaped from the improved methods would go to the money lender and not the tiller' (Mamdani, *The Myth of Population Control*). After India became independent in 1947 certain legal and financial reforms were instituted in Punjab. But until the early fifties Manupur, like many other villages, was hardly affected by them. The reason was that none of these reforms shifted the balance of power within the social structure of the village. The peasant producer remained subservient to the money lender and the economy remained unchanged. Agricultural technology was available but not relevant to life in Manupur.

Finally, in the 1950s and 60s, new systems of rural credit were established in the district of Ludhiana which did appreciably alter the balance of power in Manupur. A system of government loans was made available to all farmers which could be used not only to purchase tube wells, chemical fertilisers and wheat seeds but to repay debts. This system, together with the introduction of a new type of wheat which gave three times the previous yields, began at last to change the methods of farming in Manupur. Agricultural methods become more scientific and the outside world, with its fertilisers and machines, suddenly became either accessible or at least worth thinking about. Farmers with reasonable sized holdings were in a matter of years freed from the stranglehold of money lenders. The Brahmins who, thanks to the British, had been not merely a caste but a class, declined in economic status, and a new bourgeoisie appeared consisting of better-off farming families.

While a changed social structure was a pre-requisite to technological change, technological advances, once they began, further affected the caste structure of the village. Previously Manupur had been divided into a number of well-defined hereditary and hierarchically ordered groups or castes whose jobs, social status and economic relationships (i.e. the share they got of their own and each other's profits) were pre-determined by tradition. Now, with technological changes, a number of traditional jobs, particularly those of low caste people, became obsolete. For example, because many farming families were able to afford sewing machines, the women in these families began to make all the clothes their families needed, thus increasing their already heavy work load but at the same time putting the *Darzi* or tailor-caste workers out of employment. Finally many people of this caste had to find other non-traditional occupations. Many low caste people who had previously been craft workers turned to farm work, and as farmworkers they had to be paid not in the old feudal terms but an amount definitely related to the work they did. Labour, in other words, had become a commodity and capitalist relationships had been established in Manupur.

Among the 'lower caste' people, the woman's role had always been rather different from her role in the farming castes; now 'lower caste' women worked increasingly in the fields alongside the men and this led, according to Mamdani, to 'a radical change . . . in the attitude towards girl children . . . low caste families do not look upon the birth of a girl with the disfavour they used to' – though 'to a certain extent the disfavour persists because the girl will marry and emigrate precisely when she has reached the age of greatest productivity'.

But these social and technological changes hardly brought a more leisurely or carefree life to the farming families (who were later to be emigrants to Britain, see Table I). Production even on the smallest holdings had trebled and the work load had soared. Sons were needed – more and more sons. Without them production costs would rise because farmworkers would have to be employed and paid. Without sons, making a living out of the land would once again be impossible. The need to survive, which always dictates the moral standards of society, once more underlined the role of the women. The effect of capitalism on the women of farming families was therefore to trap them even further in their role as producers of labour power and to intensify the feeling which men and women of these families had experienced for so long that 'Life itself is work'. Leisure was something people never planned for or thought about. The land which they had loved and tended for so many generations – to survive off this land was the aim of their lives, the justification for all struggles. It was because of this that 'rest is possible only when fatigue demands it. There are no weekends, every day is a potential workday . . . rains may interrupt the activities of the men . . . but not of the women. In fact when a woman's husband is at home he demands much more and her work is increased. The major interruption to her work is pregnancy' (Mandani). But what is it like to go from one pregnancy to the next – going on having more and more children? By the age of thirty or thirty-five a woman is old and exhausted, her body bloated, her face showing the pain and suffering of her life.

Fathers, husbands and fathers-in-law are the direct tyrants of this society but their own lives are not much easier. They are brutalised by the hard and constant struggle to survive. For example, the son who is chosen by his family to go and earn money in a town and city may achieve a certain status in the joint family – he has been chosen, after all, for his abilities and strength of mind – but he has to suffer months, even years, of separation from his wife and loss of all contact with those who love him. In the city he is just another casual labourer working at the lowest level of urban employment. He can be tossed back into unemployment when he is no longer required. In the Indian sub-continent the cities have colonised the villages and the rural communities have gradually been eroded until (ideally for industrial capitalism) nothing remains but a pool of reserve labour which can be drawn upon as and when it is needed.

But capitalism, after Indian independence, was (in so far as its effects on the rural population were concerned) merely following along the paths established by British colonialism and British capitalism. Having transferred the wealth of India, Pakistan and Bangladesh to the 'mother country' Britain had left these countries at independence with a large labour force and no capital to make it productive. (It was because of this that people from the impoverished villages who sought work in the towns didn't always find it.) As a result workers could be drawn from the Indian sub-continent whenever they were required by Britain. Effectively this happened in two stages – the first in the 1920s and 30s when British colonialism wanted to create an intermediate class in East African countries, and the second after World War II when Britain in common with other Western European countries was faced with a chronic shortage of labour.

The people who emigrated in the first stage were mainly farming families from the state of Gujerat (see map) and craftworkers from Punjab, while those who came directly to Britain in the 1950s and 60s were mainly farming families from Gujerat and the Indian and Pakistani areas of Punjab. There were also smaller groups of higher and lower caste people from these areas and in addition there were people from the villages of Sylhet, a district of Bangladesh.

What I have described so far relates in general to the lives of women in the peasant communities in many parts of the Indian sub-continent, but the details I have given mainly concern women in East and West Punjab. In Gujerat these details do not always apply because the structures of communities are rather different. Rather than categorise these structures I shall describe briefly just one community, the Patels, and by tracing the changes in their dowry system, follow the changes in the position of Patel women.

The Patel community was said to have been founded around 1700, when six brothers from Persia settled in six villages in the fertile Charotar region of Gujerat. Each brother brought with him a full retinue of staff — artisans, labourers, shoemakers and so on — in fact all the elements of the Hindu caste system. The six villages (they are now small towns) each had the same structure. The landowners lived centrally, and around them, in concentric circles as it were, lived the working people. All the people in these villages called themselves Patels but they were divided into clans which corresponded quite closely with the Hindu caste system. The six brothers' direct descendants were called the *che gaon ki gor* (six village clan) and similarly the artisans and their descendants were the twelve village clan, the labourers were the twenty four village clan and right near the bottom of the caste hierarchy came the shoemakers with their clan of 'several' villages. People usually married within their own clan, and the caste system was thus maintained in the same hereditary form as in most other parts of India.

However, as elsewhere in India, with colonialism came the economic decay of the villages. In the 1920s and 30s men were forced to migrate to towns to find work. In the Patel villages the men who emigrated were mainly those from lower status groups because they were least likely to have land. There was as a result a shortage of marriageable young men among the lower Patels. This problem was solved in a manner which would be considered quite unconventional in other parts of India. Lower Patel girls married higher Patel boys but on condition that their parents paid vast dowries to acknowledge the rise in status of their daughters.

(In contrast, in other parts of India inter-caste marriages are thoroughly disapproved of.) These marriages of lower Patel girls to higher Patel boys became vast affairs, with the girl's family being forced to spend enormous sums on sweets and also give large amounts of gold to the boy's family. Not surprisingly, the position of the Patel woman changed for the worse. In lower Patel families the birth of many daughters began to be regarded as a disaster.

When the Patels emigrated to East Africa the dowry system was continued and exaggerated there. Gold became more easily available in African countries and the Patels became more and more gold-orientated as a community. East African Patels often went home to Gujerat to marry, and the women, with their vast dowries, almost invariably married higher Patels. Status, and effectively caste, was thus being bought at vast prices. In the 1950s and 60s dowries in India went down generally because gold was controlled, but not so in East Africa, where dowries rose as though they would never stop. In fact they didn't stop until the next step in Patel emigration – their expulsion from East Africa.

Perhaps it was institutions like the dowry system which made the East African Asian Patels status conscious, or maybe they used the dowry with such enthusiasm because they had become so preoccupied with status as a result of their role in East Africa. Either way, the position of women reflected by the dowry system was consistent with the Asians' new petit-bourgeois role in East Africa. In their villages of origin the women had been regarded as contributing less to the economic position of the family than the men, but they had at least been recognised as crucial to the economic life of the community. In East Africa this changed completely. As with the middle classes of Victorian England or the British colonials in India and Africa, one or two men working could maintain a large family in comfort. The women began increasingly to be regarded as possessions of their families. The marriage of a son was a way of adding to a family's wealth, and a woman's role was to display this wealth through her clothes, manner and life style. The birth of a son was welcomed now for traditional reasons (for example, among Hindus the son plays an essential part in the cremation ceremony) and because he would bring home a vast dowry when he married, but no longer so much because he would be a new worker for the joint family.

As far as the British were concerned, Asian emigration to East African countries was extremely successful. A rigid class system was established, and soon an urbanised and caste- and status-conscious bourgeoise was established which would keep the lower orders under control without demanding too much from the colonisers. In the 1950s and 60s, when Britain itself needed workers, it seemed obvious to turn again to the vast army of labour which waited in the colonies and ex-colonies, and whose situation itself had been created by colonialism.

This was how the wave of post-war emigration from Punjab, Gujerat and Bangladesh began. Men came in response to the direct demand for labour. Throughout the 1950s the size of immigration was determined by free market forces. The sort of work they were able to find was determined by economic growth and the legacy of colonial attitudes. While many indigenous workers moved up into better-paid, pleasanter and more skilled jobs, the immigrants were left the dirty, hard and low-paid work in the foundries and textile mills, as transport or catering workers or in sweat shops and small factories thrown up by the post-war boom. 'Everyone made money on the immigrant worker – from the big-time capitalist to the slum landlord – from exploiting his colour, his customs, his culture. He himself had cost the country nothing. He had been paid for by his country of origin – reared and raised as capitalist underdevelopment had willed it for the labour markets of Europe.' (A. Sivanandan, 'Race, Class and the State' in *Race & Class*, Summer 1976.) But it was this very exploitation – the fact, for example, that immigrant workers had to live in the deprived and decaying areas of big cities because of the proximity of their jobs to these areas, which led to their being regarded increasingly as undesirable. Immigration to Britain, a country of net emigration (which means that more people emigrate from it than immigrate to it) did not in itself throw up social problems but it served to highlight social deprivation. Racism became more and more intense and finally there were major eruptions in the race riots of 1958.

Up to this point the only political significance of racism had been that it provided a divided work force for employers. But after the race riots it was seen as something which the state would have both to cater for and take control of. In addition the economy was no longer so desperately short of workers. Accordingly two sets of legislation were introduced in the 1960s: the Race Relations Act, which maintained the liberal facade of the state and which, though so weak as to be almost useless in practice, had as a basis the assumption that black people were a part of the community and needed to be protected from racial prejudice: in contrast, and much more effective, were the Immigration Acts, which themselves discriminated against black workers. The 1962 Commonwealth Immigrants Act brought in a voucher system for the entry of Commonwealth citizens and distinguished between skilled and unskilled workers. This was followed by a White Paper in 1965 which discontinued vouchers for unskilled black workers though unskilled white workers were still being admitted in large numbers. These immigration laws established two important principles of future immigration policy. Firstly that Britain would never end immigration altogether (even if it ended black immigration), because if it did so the economy might not survive its periodic labour shortages. An immigrant labour force would always be needed as a buffer to absorb the shocks of alternating booms and recessions. And secondly that in the interests of 'racial harmony' the government would itself discriminate against black people and make this discrimination legal. Thus the Immigration Acts, beginning with the 1962 Act 'took discrimination out of the market place and gave it the sanction of the state. It made racism respectable and clinical by institutionalising it. In doing so it also increased the social and political consequences of racism' (A. Sivanandan, 'Race, Class and the State').

In Asian women's lives this institutionalised racism and its social consequences are of extreme importance. Apart from anything else, it was the indirect effect of these that first brought women from the Indian sub-continent to Britain. In the case of Sikh women it was the day-to-day racism which their husbands faced in Britain which indirectly brought them to Britain; with Pakistanis and Bangladeshis it was the racism of Britain's Immigration laws.

When Sikh men came to Britain in the fifties it was with the hope of making some money (usually to buy more land for the family farm) and returning. Once here, the racism they faced in employment often forced them to turn to starting their own business as a means of livelihood. (This meant borrowing money and suffering a lot of hardships; but they thought it would be worth it, because it would mean they could not be so easily discriminated against.) However, businesses take time to build up and, having built them up, and an accompanying status in the all-male Sikh society, they were reluctant to leave, and gradually more and more men started sending for their wives.

Mirpuri and Bangladeshi women came to Britain mainly as a result of immigration control. Before the 1965 Immigration Act, Mirpuri and Bengali families would send their sons to England for a few months or a few years at a time. An elder brother would come to Britain, return, and be replaced by a younger brother – and so on. The Immigration Acts with their strict control of entry made frequent trips to and from Britain impossible. Finally, the men who were here had no choice but to stay on, send for their wives and settle in Britain.

Having indirectly and inadvertently brought Asian women to Britain, the racism of the state and the racism of British society now defines the wider position of Asian women in this country – as the lowest paid and most exploited workers, or as the wives and daughters of such workers – an unstable and unacceptable situation full of conflict and contradictions. Inside their families, too, their roles are in a state of flux, with the past, the peasant past, the tribal past, the colonial past each with its own particular prescription for the woman's role constantly intruding into the present. Out of these multiple fields of conflict the future of Asian women in Britain is being resolved.

I

Isolation

'I have a burning fever – feel me, sister, feel me'

I have been married now almost twenty five years. We lived in Gulabganj (in Sylhet). My daughter married there. I have a little grandson. It was after the boy was born that I came to live in London. I came with my thirteen-year-old son to join my husband who had lived here for many, many years. It took some time to get entry, there were delays, long sessions of questioning and trouble with certificates but in the end it was sorted out and we got on a plane in April 1974. When we arrived . . . you ask me how I felt, sister . . . bad, I felt bad – to leave them all, everyone back in the village. My husband had come to collect us at the airport and we came back here in a minicar. Did I expect it to be like this? No, tell me how could I? After all I had never been here before, there was no means of knowing. I used to be sad. I used to cry, not knowing anyone or anything, missing my home . . . To live in one room after living in a country where houses are so open. It was hard, very hard.

Rezia Begum is forty one. She lives in a street near Russell Square. There is no bell on the door. To get in I and the friend who is taking me hammer and hammer on the door, shout over and over again in Bengali 'It's us, it's us, let us in'. These precautions are essential because of the danger of racial attacks. Finally Rezia throws the keys down from an upstairs window. Inside, the whole house slopes to the right, the stairs are un-washed, the walls are peeling, the door of a broken WC stands open. We go up several flights of stairs to the room where Rezia lives with her husband and son. It isn't large; two wide beds almost fill it. There is almost no other furniture. Clothes hang on a line at one side of the room. In one corner is a gas ring, in another a table with some school books on it. The room is tidy, a few pictures decorate the walls.

Rezia spends almost all her time in this room. She rarely goes out and has never been beyond the street she lives in on her own. She speaks no English and knows hardly anyone. In her first year in Britain no one visited her. Her husband is a restaurant worker. He is out all day from 11 am. to midnight. Where does he work, I ask.

'I don't know the place. I have never been there. I don't know the name or address except that it is a club of some sort. He never really talks about his work. There isn't the time.'

The isolation and emptiness of Rezia's life is typical of what many Asian women in Britain face. Those who have come from a joint family in India, Pakistan or Bangladesh to live alone with their husbands in Britain suffer most. Zubeida, a woman in her thirties, described to me her experiences of twelve years ago.

I had a proxy marriage on the telephone. My husband was here and he was a great friend of my uncle so my uncle arranged it all. . . . We stayed first in Colindale. My husband was an accountant. He was very handsome and he was very good to me. But one thing about our Asian men is that they think it a matter of pride that their women must not go out to work. But the problem for us is one of loneliness. At least if a woman goes out to work she can escape that – her mind is occupied, she does not long so much for her home in Pakistan. When I first came my husband did not want me to go out to work. It is true there was a lot of housework but I used to be very lonely. Everyday I used to cry. I missed my parents; I longed for my home and my sisters. In Pakistan they used to be my constant companions. I used to cry till my husband came home at five o'clock. Only on Saturdays and Sundays was I happy. I would make a really nice dinner, get ready and dress up. My husband would take me to a cinema. It was called the Scala. I was always waiting for Saturday.

In these lonely hours, sitting in Brick Lane in the East End or Lumb Lane in Bradford, vivid memories come flooding in from the past, from the life before this semi-existence.

Our house is open, as most houses in Sylhet are. It is made of earth and bamboo but it is beautiful. A straw thatch covers the main part, then there are verandahs and a courtyard. On moonlight nights, we, the women, used to sit there and talk or sing and prepare and eat *Pan* (betel leaf). The busiest time of the year is the rice harvest, if the crop is good that is. There used to be a lot of work. I and other girls and women, we'd work the *Dhenki*, husking the rice, or sometimes we'd go to the fields carrying tobacco and food for my brothers-in-law and cousins who were working there. Occasionally we'd harvest the lighter crops, like sweet potatoes or chillis. Then the rainy season would come. When the rains come to my country the clusters of houses are like islands. Here and there a tall *Tal* tree (a kind of palm) stands out, all else is submerged. When I was a young girl I and my sisters would get a boat and slip away, visiting friends from island to island. Of course the elders didn't like it, they thought we were tomboys, but we loved it – the sound of the water, the rocking and splashing. . . . Sometimes at night, the music of boatmen would come floating up, blown by the waves and wind, a flute playing the music of the river. Why, why did I ever leave my home?

In London it is 4 pm. Outside the evening is drawing in already. Rezia is waiting for her son to come home from school. She is worried about him. About a month ago he was severely beaten up by a gang of white boys on the way back from school.

They used to bully him and tease him; then one day on his way back from school they attacked him. The next day he and another Bengali boy who lives near by chose another way home, hoping to escape the attackers. But the gang found out and followed him here. Just as my son entered our room I could see them, seven or eight hefty white boys entering through the door downstairs. We could hear them coming up the stairs right to our door and then shouting and hammering on it. I got up and quietly bolted the door. We kept very still inside and in the end we could hear them slowly going down the stairs and going away. After that I did not want my son to go to school but in the end some Bengali men in the area took it up with the Headmaster and since then there has been no trouble.

A community worker who helped the family told me:

We took it up with the Education Officer who asked for information about the family. I told them I know them well, their son is not the type who just gets in fights. When it was taken up with the Headmaster he said that the boy's name was not on the roll, they did not know of him. We felt he was trying to avoid the whole issue. Anyway in the end he and the Education Officer did take some action to control the bullies and since then there has been no trouble. But just think if the family had not been in touch with the Bengali Action Group or with any community workers, what sort of state of fear they'd live in. And there are many families like that. The police? – who would call them, these families don't have telephones. And even if they are called they hardly ever come in time.

Many other women I spoke to told me that for protection from racial attacks it was essential to have Asian neighbours. Calling the police had proved again and again to be useless. During the racial violence of summer 1976, a housewife from Newham told me:

It was just an ordinary evening. I had done all the cooking and was waiting for my husband to come home. Suddenly I heard a loud scream and rushed to the front door. Half a dozen white teenagers were beating someone up. There was blood on the pavement. I couldn't see who it was at first, then I realised it was my husband. He was unconscious on the ground. They were kicking and beating him. I screamed for help. The neighbours rushed out and we beat off the thugs with sticks and broom handles. We called the police and ambulance but it was a long time before the police arrived. They went to see my husband in hospital and asked him to see them when he came out. But when he did they showed no interest at all, they just said the officer concerned was not there. They made no attempt to catch the thugs.

This family had Asian neighbours. Below is the story of a Bengali family in the East End who did not (*Guardian* 6.6.77):

In Shadwell Gardens, by Cable Street there is a large block of council flats. On the ground floor my interpreter from the Bengali Housing Association led the way into a small, bare flat inhabited by a Bengali widow with three children of six, eight and nine.

Last Saturday night they were watching television. They had just had the windows repaired from the last volley of stones. Fists started hammering on their windows. They turned the lights out and sat in fear.

They heard sounds in the kitchen: breaking glass, sounds of unknown things coming into their home. Peeking around the kitchen door, they saw rubbish being emptied from dustbins into their home. Then a stone came through the living room window. The widow gathered her children and ran out of the front door seeking protection from another Bengali family thirty yards across the court.

There were about thirty people waiting for them as they left their home. The bruises on the neck and face and legs of the widow and her children were still livid on the brown skin as they recounted how they had run a gauntlet of fists and kicks and curses of their neighbours.

Yelling in Bengali for help, they reached the door of the other family. One of its sons came out and tried to help them inside. He was pulled into the court and beaten on the face. He stood beside the broken glass of his front door as he described how the white neighbours – assisted by two West Indian girls – hauled him into the court and beat him. The bruises and lumps were still fresh and unhealed on his face.

The police arrived three hours later, by which time the seige of the Bengali homes had ended . . . Bengali families in the East End feel they have no protection and that they must begin to protect themselves. They say that the police could stop the violence overnight if the Special Patrol Group was assigned to patrol the area, or if the Home Office made it sufficiently clear that this kind of activity must stop. One of the fears of the Bengali community is that the new Conservative administration of the GLC will not honour a private agreement reached with the Labour GLC in 1976, for quick and emergency relocation of harassed Asian families.

If these fears prove justified, it won't be the first time Asian families would be forced through deliberate government policies to live in terrifying isolation. Right from the early 1960s the attitude of local authorities and housing departments has been that 'ghettos' must be avoided at all costs, and even a handful of Asian families can make an area into a ghetto. (Councillor Harry Doran, Newham, reported in the *Newham Recorder*, May 1976 – 'The estate is becoming a ghetto. Only eight floors (of a tower block) are without an immigrant family'.)

When in 1972 the Uganda Asians started coming to Britain, the government's Uganda Resettlement Board operated a deliberate policy of dispersal. Refugee families in obvious distress were discouraged and often prevented from joining their relations and Asian friends in Britain by the Board's refusal of all aid to them if they settled in areas with significant Asian populations. This has led to situations like that described in *A Job Well Done?* by Helene Middleweek and Michael Ward, a report prepared on behalf of the Co-ordination Committee for the Welfare of Evacuees from Uganda, of a family consisting of mother, father and thirteen-year-old son, where neither of the parents spoke any English and the father was almost paralysed. They were settled in a remote area of Ross and Cromarty in Scotland, twenty miles from the nearest Asian family.

Isolation is seen from the outside as a result of women not speaking English, or of their being forced to stay at home for cultural reasons. But it is much more than this. It is a state of mind, one of shock and withdrawal. Weakened by the separation from their families, suffering often the loss of mother, sisters and close friends, these Asian women find themselves in a strange unknown society. The realisation that this is a racist society, a society which wishes them dead for the colour of their skin, accentuates their loneliness, and their isolation in turn makes it harder for them to fight against racism.

Living in the conditions I have described can cause the strongest personalities to sink into depression. For pregnant women, or those who have just had babies, the pressures are sometimes so great that they become mentally disturbed.

Post-natal depression is said to be common among immigrant women generally. Among Asians it affects particularly those who are separated from their families. Indigenous British women affected by post-natal depression are often single mothers or those whose husbands or boyfriends don't give them the care and affection or help they need in this new stage of their life. For Asian women, separation from their families can cause the same torment. Often these women, sometimes as young as seventeen or eighteen, suffer alone, no one except their husbands knows about them, or cares. Occasionally they are referred to hospitals, but the treatment they receive sometimes serves only to underline their isolation.

A London hospital allowed me to visit one of their patients. She was Manisha, a Muslim girl of twenty from Sylhet, and had just had her second child. She had been having fits of anger, and had been neglecting her children, I was told. She was being treated at home at that time. A community nurse was visiting her so that she wouldn't get too lonely and depressed. This nurse, I was surprised to discover, was a man. He seemed a very pleasant person but he spoke no Bengali. In fact he said to me 'You could be quite useful, you know, you could help me get through to her.'

We went to see Manisha one winter afternoon. The nurse had brought along a male friend of his. Manisha lived in a council flat in a decrepit estate. Garbage littered the outside; a very old white woman hobbled slowly on crutches into a downstairs flat. As we entered the building a white woman leaning from a balcony screamed a stream of abuse. We went up to the second floor and knocked at Manisha's flat. For a long time there was no sound inside, then the door opened. A Bengali girl, absurdly young, stood there holding a baby in her arms. She didn't look at us, didn't answer when I spoke in Bengali. Finally, still silent, she turned and led us into the main room. She left us there a few minutes, then, coming to the door, beckoned me to the next room. There at last she began to speak. This is how I remember it.

My head aches all the time. I have a burning fever – feel me sister, feel me. Inside me sometimes is such anger, anger with my babies, with my husband, with the whole of my life. Then suddenly I am panic-stricken. My head fells as though it is on fire. It started when I got home from hospital after having my baby. My husband gave me the news that my father had died back in the village. Now, thinking of them, how do I feel . . . Late, late at night my husband comes home. He loves the babies. He is a good husband, but what can he do? And what can I do? How can I live, sister, how can I live!

In the next room the nurse and his friend were playing with Manisha's older child.

What was it that Manisha was missing so desperately? Ranu, a Sylheti woman in her late twenties, told me of the enveloping love and care a woman with her first or second child can receive in Bangladesh.

If a girl is lucky and her parents are alive, she goes to her mother's house for the last few months of her pregnancy and about the first three months of the baby's life. There she gets a lot of love and care. She is asked 'What would you like to eat? What do you fancy?' All the time she is looked after. The whole matter of pregnancy is one of celebration. When the baby is born it is an occasion of joy for the whole family. The naming ceremony is so lovely. It is held when the baby is seven days old. A new dress is bought for it and a new sari for the mother. There is feasting and singing till late at night. The women and young girls gather and sing songs. Garlands of turmeric and garlic are worn to ward off evil spirits. That's when the name is chosen. The *Maulvi* of course selects a formal Arabic name, but the celebration I am telling you about involves choosing a name to call the child by. Suggestions are asked for from the family and friends all over the village.
Then a new cane *Kulo* (tray for dusting rice) is taken, a big one with pictures woven into it perhaps, and the names are written on it in ink. Candles are placed by each name. The name which burns the longest is chosen. The same ceremony is held for the birth of a boy or a girl. Of course it is considered better to have a boy, but the birth of a girl is celebrated with the same joy by the women in the family. We sit together eating *pan* and singing. Some of us

might be young unmarried girls, others aged ladies of 40 or 50. There are so many jokes, so much laughter. People look so funny eating *pan* and singing. The men don't take much part. They may come and have a look at the baby, but the singing, the gathering together at night – it is all women. The songs are simple songs which are rarely written down. They are about the lives of women in Bengal.

Back in London, what is available to mentally disturbed women who are treated in hospital? I cannot make generalisations without a far more detailed study of hospitals. But it is worth mentioning what a very experienced and established psychiatrist told me about his work when I interviewed him. When I asked how he communicated with Bengali patients who spoke no English he said 'I have no trouble in communicating with them because I learned pidgin English in the army.' What were the main illnesses people suffered from? I asked. He replied:

Well, at certain times we have had a large number of Bengali patients. In fact at one time before the Pakistan-Bangladesh war there were so many that we called this form of depression Pakistani Syndrome. The symptoms were bleary eyes, pain in the head, loss of weight, sleeplessness, and for the men impotency. We gave electric treatment. Some had it twice. But if they came more than once their friends usually sent them home. After two bouts they go home; they don't recover. During the war it was better. There were very few patients. The war took people's minds off things. Now again there is less psychiatry because people are afraid of losing their jobs. Living conditions don't affect them. They do adapt, they are jolly and supportive.

As for the women, he said, they suffered from the same sort of things – depression and sometimes guilt. He told me of one case he had had of a woman in her early twenties. Her own family were in Bangladesh. Her husband, a restaurant owner, was almost twice her age and diabetic. She was acutely depressed and had a pain in the back of her neck. He had treated her for several months using her husband as an interpreter – as though her husband were an objective witness to her depression. He told me;

It took me time to find out what was wrong but eventually I sorted it out. The patient had been living before she came to London on the outskirts of a town in Bangladesh. She never wore the veil.

One day an older woman who wore the veil cursed her and accused her of being loose. This curse resulted in guilt, because in a way you see it was true. She was loose. For example every day when the came to see me she wore a beautiful new sari.

I found this account sad but also rather revealing. It showed not only a lot of racism and sexist vanity on the part of the psychiatrist but ignorance about the way of life of his patient. That young girl hardly out of her teens, married to an ailing elderly man, probably never went out of the house apart from these visits to the hospital. Being well-off (the wife of a restaurant owner), she had many beautiful saris. Wearing a different one every time she went out would be only normal, particularly since a sari does not have to be washed as frequently as a dress because it is not worn next to the skin.

To get a more general view of how the Health Service departments treat their Asian women patients, I asked social workers in different parts of London what their experiences had been in dealing with hospitals, Health Visitors and Area Health Authorities. They told me that there were serious everyday problems which arose because the needs of Asian patients were being ignored. There is, for example, a general absence of interpreters in hospitals even in areas with high immigrant populations. Some terrifying situations occur as a result. There was the case, for example, of a five-year-old boy who was taken to hospital vomiting violently and with a high temperature. It was two days before medical staff found out what his distraught parents were trying to tell them – that he had swallowed the contents of a tin of paint.

The hospital staff I spoke to were almost without exception complacent on the subject of interpreters. In one hospital in an area with a large proportion of Bangladeshis, the Hospital Secretary told me 'We rarely need interpreters but we have a list of members of staff who speak various foreign languages' – for Bengali there was a porter and a cook – both male.

In Wandsworth the attitude of the Area Health Authority and of Health Visitors was described to me by Geeta Amin, a social worker with Wandsworth Community Relations Council.

We wanted to do a research project on the reasons for the low take-up of Health Clinics and Health Services by Asian women. It seemed to be a very important project but the Area Health Authority felt it would be 'unethical'. There is a complete lack of

understanding, and that goes right the way through the Health
Service . . . I have been giving a series of seminars on nutrition
and the Asian family to Health Visitors. I have been telling them
about the different sensitivity which Asian women have to their
babies and the fact that you can't just go up to an Asian woman
with the diet leaflet and say you should be giving your baby Cod
Liver Oil, because 90 per cent of Asians in Wandsworth are
vegetarians. But one faces a continuous battle with these Health
Visitors. You go to a seminar and say 'Listen, they don't eat this
kind of thing!' But their attitude remains the same – 'Well we treat
them all the same whether they are Asian or English'. That is the
fundamental policy of all social services – 'We treat them all the
same. We don't see any difference. If we can tell an English
mother to do that we'll tell an Asian mother to do that.'

Something which shows the Area Health Authority policy is
their refusal to have any special facilities for Asian women. They
complain that Asian women don't attend clinics for mother's
groups and discussions. But they are not interested in the reasons
for it, in the sort of alienation which Asian women feel at these
groups. We suggested a special Asian mother's group to discuss
health problems. They said 'We can't have anything of the sort,
we don't run separate facilities for Asians, and not only that, we
are not going to allow you to use the Health Clinic for anything
that is solely for Asians.'

Hashmat Ara Begum, a community worker in the Borough of
Camden told me that she too had come across the most
contemptuous attitudes among Health Visitors. She said that they
seemed to regard Asian women as ignorant and stupid people
who neglected their children. She explained why Bangladeshi
women sometimes found it difficult to look after their children in
Britain.

What young mothers suffer from more than almost anything else
is having constant responsibility for their children. In Bangladesh
children under the age of five or six are looked after by the whole
family. All the children in the joint family are looked after
together. They are taken to the pond for a bath perhaps by one
daughter-in-law, and she baths them all. Then they all come in
and sit down to eat. Perhaps the youngest daughter-in-law has
cooked the meal. Another woman feeds them. As for playing,
children play out of doors with natural objects. Here people say
that Asian children don't play with toys. In Bangladesh they don't

need toys. They make their own simple things – models and castles out of mud, dolls with red earth and leaves. Being out of doors means they are not always cooped up in one room with their mothers. In the afternoon or evening they love to hear *Rupkotha* (fairy tales). Maybe there is a favourite aunt, she tells them these stories. But at night when they get sleepy they always go to their mother and sleep in her embrace. But other women do help a lot, in fact they have such strong relationships with the child that it is not uncommon for them to be called Big Mother or Small Mother. Here, in Britain, the attitude of women is quite different; they may say why should another woman look after my baby or even touch my baby.

Snatched from the security and love of their sisters in the joint family, Bengali women in Britain often find themselves forced into total emotional dependence on their husbands. For many it is a strange and difficult experience, one which people who have always lived in a nuclear family find hard to understand. In fact their feelings and the vast emotional adjustment they have to make are perhaps best explained to nuclear family dwellers by considering the reverse transplant from nuclear to joint family. For Asian women coming to join their husbands in Britain the experience is if anything more bewildering; first, the change is permanent: then, often enough there are also the problems of racism and poverty. But how do those western women feel, for example, who having lived with their Indian husbands in Britain for years, are suddenly thrust into the bosom of the joint family, even temporarily. This is how Janet described her three-month visit to her husband's family in an Indian village in Bihar:

I found it really hard when I was left totally to the women's company . . . One of the things I didn't like too much was the terrific hullabaloo the women made about menstruation, the way they would sit sighing in a corner and all the other women would make a fuss over them. As a feminist I wanted these women to stop having what seemed to me to be silly attitudes . . . They were terribly puzzled by me. They often asked me if I had a baby in my tummy because they saw no evidence of my menstruation . . . These women don't have a role of status or power in society. So when they are sick, especially women's things, they make the most of it. For example, during pregnancy and just after you are queen for ten or eleven months. When I was sick I experienced a great deal of love and consideration. But I found I could communicate better with men. One particular uncle, he showed such warmth that a western man would find it very hard to show. With the women it was less easy. They often stroked and embraced each other and me. I could sense their warmth and desire to please but I didn't know how to respond. A lot of the day they sat round the oven talking. I would attempt to do something like peeling potatoes with one of those footknives. This would be a source of pleasure to them. But often I hated spending time with them. It was frighteningly boring.

While it is true that village women in India have little power or status in society as a whole, Janet misunderstands what lies behind the caring and 'fussing'. It is not as she thinks a desire to 'make the most of it', to somehow claim importance, but rather a recognition that in this oppressive society women need the care and emotional support of other women.

Often Asian women coming from joint families in the Indian subcontinent to join their husbands in Britain do succeed in making the necessary emotional adjustment, but for many of them it takes months if not years; for some coping with the total emotional dependence on the husband alone is just not possible. I do not mean of course that there is no tradition of love in marriage. The oldest stories in Indian mythology are after all love stories, accounts of the relationships of lovers, and specifically of married couples. The same is true of Urdu poetry. In the villages of Bangladesh the folk-songs, even the tapestries women make, tell stories of love and romance. What I do mean is that although most women do hope for a happy and loving relationship with their husbands, the attainment of this is not the purpose of marriage. The role of marriage which acts as a conservative force, is economic and childbearing, and the knowledge of this role hangs like a dark shadow over any possible relationships. For the girl, marriage does not then symbolise a heightened or new relationship with a man. It means instead the end of childhood and freedom, the beginning of a new life as a slave and chattel at the bottom of a hierarchy in someone else's family. 'One day,' as one Pakistani girl in Bradford said, 'I was a child playing out of doors, the next I was a married woman with a life full of work.' To symbolise her new life, her new role defined for her by the male rule-makers of society, a girl may even be given a new name on marriage.

For village women in Punjab, Bengal or Gujerat, there is

usually only one source of comfort in their new life – the presence of other women – to love them, caress them, sing songs with them and soothe their sorrows. In Britain, for these women who live alone with their husbands, this comfort is lacking, the afternoon hour spent lying on a bed chatting with their sisters-in-law, combing and oiling each other's hair, is replaced by empty hours sitting by the heater in some grey suburb. Often their husbands are much older than them, not so much for traditional reasons as because men settled in Britain are considered of higher status and class and therefore, being more desirable as sons-in-law, they can find young brides. As one Bengali girl bitterly commented: 'You may have wondered why among Sylheti families in this area (King's Cross) the man is often horribly old with a crooked face while his wife is a young girl of astonishing beauty. That's because parents in Sylhet seem to think it is a big deal, a real status symbol to get a *Biliti Bor* (a bridegroom from England).'

Another woman told me about how Sylheti men returned to the village to find a bride: 'After years in England they suddenly decide to marry a village girl. They go, in their smart suits and ties, back to the village. The villagers hold them in awe and think of them as men of the world. People don't know about London. Don't know what a rotten life their daughter will have.'

Often the men marry girls not only younger but of a higher social class than their own in Sylhet. Back in London in the Sylheti community, having a young, good-looking wife from a comparatively high class is in turn a status symbol. The next step, which only the most well-off men such as restaurant owners can afford, is keeping this wife in semi-purdah – in other words sentencing her to solitary confinement.

This greed for status reinforces the wife's role as child-bearing domestic slave or chattel, and spoils for ever the chance of a real relationship. Any error on her part, however small, and he may remind her that he can go back to Bangladesh and marry again. Any gynaecological illness, even a Caesarian operation, and he may regard her as unfit for sex and therefore useless: and he will go back to Bangladesh and marry again. Two Bengali women in their twenties told me of many women they knew, and knew of, who were thus stranded. 'After that' said one of them 'how can there be any love between husband and wife. The husband, loving him, looking after him is regarded by us as a duty. He may be like a banana tree or a coconut tree, half human in appearance, revolting in every way, but caring for him is still a woman's duty if he's her husband. At home (in Bangladesh) we can balance it out in our minds because of all the love and happiness we can get from the women in the family. Here, all that is in the past we yearn for.'

II
The Family
'A part of myself . . . which gives me so much pain'

'My family is like a part of myself, of my body; if I cut it off I could die. But it is a part which gives me so much pain that sometimes I can't bear it – can't bear it at all.'

Asian women come from many different language groups, practise at least three main religions and have come to Britain in varied patterns of migration – but ask them about their family life and the similarity of their experience stands out like the skeleton in an X-ray. Their lives are dominated by three main concepts – the male ego whose nurturing, preserving and boosting is considered of vital importance; a sense of hierarchy which is considered synonymous with the existence of the family; and finally the closeness of relationships – the bonds which provide consolation. These three concepts were also basic to women's lives in the villages of India, Pakistan and Bangladesh; they were principles essential to the societies they lived in. In Britain these principles are still present but meaningless, their very irrelevance making their upholders all the more determined and aggressive.

The structures and sizes of Asian families in Britain vary, depending to a certain extent on their regional background in the Indian subcontinent. Among Sikhs, for example, many of the first male immigrants arrived in the 1950s, by the 60s they had been joined by their wives and children and by the 70s many of them had brought their elderly parents. These large families – two or three brothers, their wives and children and their parents – usually live in one house. Among Mirpuri Muslims, in most cases the family consists of husband and wife, their children, and a network of cousins living not necessarily in one house but in one neighbourhood, as in the Lumb Lane area of Bradford. Among Bangladeshis, often enough it is a husband and wife and their sons of various ages, the daughters being left with the joint family in Bangladesh which from there casts its light and shadow on the lives of Bengali women in Britain. As for the Gujeratis from East Africa, in many cases the whole joint family has been transplanted into Britain, from young babies even to great grandmothers. The whole joint family is on the scene, bearing the onslaught of British society and groaning with agony as a result – groaning on the one hand because of the intense racism and poverty it faces and on the other because of the confusions caused by the irrelevance in Britain of its most valued concepts.

There are of course other groups of Asian immigrants, Punjabis from East Africa, urban immigrants from towns like Delhi and so on. But I will not mention here every group of Asian immigrants in Britain, nor analyse every family structure, but present what the Asian women I spoke to told me about their feelings and situations. Here I shall try to describe certain aspects of family life for three main groups of women – Punjabi and Pathan Muslims from Pakistan, Sikhs from India and Gujerati Hindus from East Africa.

It is often said that Muslim men think it a matter of pride that their women shouldn't work. If it is thought that this is one of the pleasanter, more protective aspects of male chauvinism, this is mistaken. 'Work' in this statement does not include housework, ill-paid home sewing or the heavy work of carrying food to the fields in Pakistan. What Muslim men don't like is for their women to work outside the home, potentially in the company of strange men. But to ascribe this to male chauvinism wouldn't be accurate either. These attitudes are created by *Izzat*, the sensitive and many-faceted male family identity which can change as the situation demands it – from family pride to honour to self respect, and sometimes to pure male ego.

Predictably, it is women who can place Izzat most easily at risk. In the villages of Pakistan, a woman working outside her home does not usually come across men unrelated to her and because of this, group or family identity is not endangered. As Farda, a girl from the Jhelum area told me, 'in the village everyone is our *Biradiri* (brethren). So women don't need to wear *Burkhas* to avoid being seen by strange men. But in towns, even in small towns it is not the same. People from different families live and work in the same area and as a result women are forced into *Burkhas*.' For this reason urban women in Pakistan only rarely work outside the home. Salima a woman from a small provincial town told me:

If a girl has a job, relatives and neighbours start saying of their family – 'What kind of people are they, have they no *Izzat* to make their daughter work?' If she is an educated girl you might think there would be careers open to her but only three are available – teacher, doctor or nurse (although even nursing is disapproved of). If she is a teacher in a girl's school and even one man is employed there, people start saying there is a man there among the women. If she has to deal with him at all, even quite briefly, people start saying 'She's always talking to that man, – who knows why she has so much to say.' So you see it isn't easy for a woman to keep a job.

However, despite this, in Britain 21 per cent of Muslim women do work outside the home. It is because, as Salima, herself a factory worker, explained to me 'the money is needed and not only that, there is a feeling among some people that what you do in Britain doesn't really count.'

But Izzat, with its centuries long history, its emotional pull towards India and Pakistan, is not so easily dealt with. Rational arguments and the need for money may keep it submerged but from time to time it is so inflamed that it can no longer be suppressed. It surfaces, bringing feelings of humiliation and chagrin and causing conflict in the family. British society serves in fact to keep Izzat alive. The contempt for Asian culture, the constant shadow of racial hostility and the disregard for family and group identity provide an atmosphere in which Izzat is constantly at risk and therefore is constantly charged and re-charged. As a result the women suffer; they are made the scape-goats of damaged Izzat. It is they, after all, who have always been the symbols of their culture and traditionally it is at their slightest touch that the delicate flower of Izzat can shrivel.

In Britain Izzat faces a whole new range of threats. Should girls brought up in Britain be allowed to go on to further education? Should they be allowed to take jobs? Can their marriages be delayed? Each one of these issues can be regarded in orthodox families as having an effect on Izzat. Often they are questions on which the hierarchy of the family (in so far as it exists in Britain) has to be consulted. And their group view is frequently more conservative than that of any one member. The group gives support to those whose Izzat has been injured and suggests repressive remedies. The women who face this repression have no such support.

The Pathan community in Bradford provides many such examples of community and family interaction where the net result is the oppression of women. In Bradford the Pathans live mainly in extended families in large houses in the Hanover Square area. The married women are rarely to be seen outside. When they visit their friends they travel by back alleys from house to house. To that extent their village life in Pakistan is mirrored in Bradford. But they have children – daughters who go to school in Britain. What happens when these daughters grow up? This case was described to me by Hamida Kazi, a community worker in Bradford.

I had a case of a Pathan family where the husband used to beat his wife all the time. There was nowhere on her body which wasn't black with bruises. Even her eyes had blood on them. 'Even if I am sleeping,' she told me 'at 12 o'clock at night he comes and pulls the quilt off and starts beating me'. I asked why? Was she a bad cook? She said 'No, he likes my cooking and I keep the house very tidy.' It is a sort of cultural conflict which must have been going on in the husband's mind. Pathans are very very orthodox and sometimes religious fanatics. This couple have four or five kids and their eldest daughter is about seventeen. She is very beautiful and intelligent. She is doing 'O' levels and wants to do 'A' levels. He wants her to get married instead. He thinks she should go to Pakistan because if she doesn't she'll get her own way. One day he stabbed his wife in the hand. His ten-year-old son got so frightened he ran and called the police. The police came and he was taken away. The underlying cause of all this was the girl's future. When I went to see the family, the mother was very rational and calm and the girl told me: 'there must be millions like me, Mrs Kazi. I want to be a social worker so I could do something for these girls.' The father was remanded in custody for one week. The police inspector told me: 'When he comes out he'll probably go straight home and attack her.' So I tried my best and managed to get a council house for her to move into. I asked her to move out at once. But after I left, all the people from the Pathan community came to see her. They forced her not to accept the house. They told her that if she did they would outcast her. That was too much of a price to pay. She told me what they had said – that it is a loss of honour, 'It is disrespectful to your husband.' I said 'Where the hell were they when he was beating you? Isn't it disrespectful for man to beat his wife?'

The answer to that of course is 'no'; because honour, pride and ego are always assumed to be male. Married women may sometimes feel that they share the Izzat of their family but they are aware that in reality Izzat belongs to the men of the family. A wife's role is to nurture this Izzat and bring up her children so that they too understand and respect it. It was here presumably that the Pathan woman had erred. But to succeed in this particular role is if anything more difficult in Britain than it was in Pakistan. Often a mother can understand her daughter's needs, if not in detail at least in broad terms, and at the same time she knows that these needs are in conflict with traditional honour and respectability.

What it is like for a daughter in these circumstances is described by Afshan Begum (a young Muslim woman who grew up in Britain) in her thesis *Adolescent Muslim girls in British Schools*.

The relationship between the Muslim girl and her mother is a very important one. Often on coming from school tired, she takes consolation in the fact that her mother seems content and happy in her role – maybe there is a chance she will be too . . . parents often have few outside contacts . . . the mother especially tries to obtain most of her emotional satisfaction from her children. The demands on the children are increased if the father spends a great deal of his leisure time with his men friends . . . Girls often become very close to their mothers, consequently the last thing they want to do is to bring any form of unhappiness to their lives.

For a Muslim girl trapped in this situation, running away from home is only a painful last resort:

She has to think of her younger sisters, her father may clamp down on what little freedom they had previously. Not only will her mother feel immense unhappiness about the action her daughter has taken but there is also the chance that her father may take unpleasant measures and throw harsh accusations at her for not having brought up her daughter properly. It will be considered her mother's fault not only by her husband but by the community also.

Family honour and pride, which are so easily upset by a woman's actions, are far less easily affected by a man's errors. A married man's promiscuity, for example, leaves his family Izzat in impeccable condition. Many of the Muslim women I spoke to told me that their husbands were unfaithful to them usually with white women (see for example p. 123 of 'Sisters in Struggle'). This letter written to the *Daily Jang*, an established Urdu newspaper printed in Britain, shows how the family responds to a man's promiscuity.

I am twenty years old and have been educated in Britain. At eighteen I had taken three 'O' levels and 2 'A' levels in secretarial subjects. I very much wanted to continue with my studies but had to get married in accordance with my parents' wishes. A few months after my marriage, I was told by my in-laws that, following the teachings of Islam, I would have to obey them in every way. This meant that I couldn't lead my own life at all; when I complained about this to my husband he laughed it off. Later I found out that my husband was being unfaithful to me. When I spoke about this problem to my parents-in-law they only laughed. Eventually, when I was sure of my husband's adultery, I left him, taking my one-year-old daughter. Though I respect the teachings of Islam I don't understand how there can be one law for men and another for women. While I was supposed to be at the beck and call of not only my husband but even his parents, his going around with other women was just taken for granted.

In contrast, if a married woman were unfaithful to her husband she might have to die for Izzat to be restored.

Once Izzat is tainted a woman can do very little about it. In Pakistan, family feuds are fought out between men. They drag on from generation to generation and emigration to Britain makes very little difference. The women watch in silence or, as chattels, suffer the consequences. Take the experience of Jamila, a girl from a very rural part of Azad Kashmir.

Her family had come to Bradford when she was about fourteen. At sixteen they had her married to a cousin who lived about a mile away. Soon after, her husband's family in Pakistan and her own family there were torn apart by a feud. Someone had backed out of a marriage and family honour had been damaged. Word of the feud arrived in Britain with astonishing speed. There were beatings up in Bradford and brawls in Accrington. At the time Jamila had been married, her husband's brother had also been married to a girl named Zahira. The four of them lived in one house with the father of the two men. After the feud he refused to allow Jamila to visit her parents. She used to spend her whole day locked in a basement room with her sister-in-law and the four young children they had between them. The husbands worked upstairs in the shop the family owned. A friend who used to visit them occasionally told me what conditions were like:

It was very damp in the cellar. They sat by the fire all the time. It was not that they were there as a punishment, just that the cellar was their living room (a common arrangement in the back-to-backs of Bradford where most Asian families live). Jamila said that her husband was a good man, he didn't beat her, but she was unhappy because she was never allowed out to visit her parents

and brother and sister. Most of the day Jamila and Zahira chatted
to each other. Sometimes they knitted beautiful cardigans with
patterns similar to fair-isle. But they were depressed and
demoralised. They did the cooking between them, but the food
was meagre and monotonous. The kitchen was a stone room off
the cellar. It was very cold and damp and was completely under
the house with no windows. It had an ancient cooker and sink.
There was a high wall round the house and there was a yard.
Jamila and Zahira were allowed into the yard to hang their
washing but they couldn't sit there chatting. They were lucky
because they had each other. They seemed devoted to each other.
Their main pleasure seemed to be in the beautiful garments they
made for each other and for their children.

Making clothes for each other is a traditional pleasure for
Pakistani women. It is a physical demonstration of the closeness
of the joint family. In Britain, Pakistani women continue to
enthuse over the fashions in *Salwar Kamiz* which reach London
from Pakistan, usually via Bradford.

What is often dismissed rather contemptuously as baggy
trousers and tunic by English people exists in fact in a variety of
styles. Older Kashmiri women stick to the traditional Kashmiri
form where the *Kamiz* (or the *Kurta* as it is called in Kashmir) is
rather long, usually with a distinct waist, and the trousers are full,
almost bulbous, with a deep and stiff cuff at the ankle. Teenage
girls or young wives like Jamila and Zahira try out the new
fashions coming in from Pakistan.

What was the latest style to arrive in London, I asked three
young Muslim women from Mirpur who live in a North London
suburb. 'Just now,' they told me 'it is the *Garara* (trousers which
flare from just above the knee) and quite a short *Kamiz* to go with
it and of course a *Dupatta* (a long light scarf) in georgette in an
exactly matching colour'.

These three were lighthearted girls, always laughing and joking
together in loud, unselfconscious voices. Each was the sister-in-
law of the other and they lived in suburban semis on adjacent
streets. Fazila and Salima attended English classes but Ruksana
was forbidden to by her father-in-law who thought she had too
much to do in the house. She was in fact not only a housewife but
a homeworker, sewing blouses at 35p a piece. She made between
70 and 90 blouses a week which, despite the low rate of pay,
compares well with what she might have got as a part-time

worker in a sweat shop, the most likely alternative. 'If I get lonely,' she told me 'I ring up Fazila and Salima and they come and help me with my sewing.'

I had arranged to meet them at Salima's house, but when I got there she told me that the other two were at Ruksana's place. She would take me there but could I wait while she changed her clothes. When she returned she was dressed in plain creamy pink trousers flared all the way, a short *Kamiz* of the same colour but with a pattern of small gold stars and a matching *Dupatta*.

The *Kamiz* material was called Rathkirani or queen of the night.

Any young woman may enjoy following the latest fashions, but for Pakistani women there is a difference in their attitude to clothes. Unlike western fashion clothes, whose form and variations are dependent on business interests, these Pakistani garments are created especially for the wearer by a joint effort of the women of the family. They are enjoyed in a sense by the whole family. This is a characteristic of all Indian cultures. In my own family in India, often enough saris are bought for me by my father or mother. I wear them for my own enjoyment but equally for theirs. A young woman going to buy material for her Salwar Kamiz in Bradford or Newham would almost invariably be accompanied by her mother or husband or cousin or at least a friend. They would go to an Indian or Pakistani shop, since the sort of cloth needed is not easily available in ordinary department stores.

You don't go in and say – I want three yards of this. You talk to the man you are buying it from and he really takes trouble over you. You can take your time, touch the material, hold it up against you, take it to the door and look at it. They don't think you are going to steal it, and they never tell your children off if they touch things or run in and out of the hanging displays.

When you have bought the material, if you own a machine you make it up with help from everyone else in your family. Gina Skelton, an English school teacher, described to me how women in a traditional Muslim family made a Kamiz for her.

I had some material and they said they would make it up into a Kamiz for me, so next time I went there I took along a garment that fitted me. We laid it out on the floor and they measured it up. The two girls who were near my age cut the material. They asked me how I wanted the neck and slits. Everyone took an interest. The mother watched, the little sister watched and the men came in now and then and offered advice.

Salwar Kamiz is like a national dress of Punjab, worn both by the Muslims of Pakistan and Hindus and Sikhs of East Punjab in India. There are differences of style and certain colours are favoured by one group more than by the others but these differences are small. The symbolic meaning of the clothes is the same for all Punjabis.

The Dupatta (or *Chunni* as Hindus and Sikhs call it) is the most obviously symbolic part of a woman's clothes. Its function is basically to cover a woman's hair and hide the shape of her breasts but it can be worn in a variety of ways, draped round the top half of her body and head, folded over her chest and hanging over her shoulders or loosely placed round her neck. The way she wears it shows to the righteous and inquisitive observers always present in Asian communities just how modest she is. In Pakistan, 'if you see a girl with her Dupatta pushed up and her limbs in a relaxed position, standing and talking to boys, people passing will go on staring and start whispering among themselves – "Where is her modesty!" or, "what is going on there!" They'll turn their heads and stare.' In Britain the attitude remains the same but the Dupatta is not quite so essential. Sometimes it has to be abandoned for convenience or because of a changed lifestyle. As Sabra, a woman in her forties, told me 'If I go out I usually do have my Dupatta round me, but at work I can't wear it in case it gets caught up in the machines, so I just wear a scarf on my head when I leave the house –something is needed to save one's Izzat'.

Wearing a Dupatta over one's head is also a sign of respect for elders (and for God: a Sikh woman entering a *Gurdwara* (Sikh temple) always covers her head with a Dupatta). A new bride is expected to cover her head in the presence of her parents-in-law and older brothers-in-law. Whether she does this or not depends, in Britain, on her own personality and on the attitude of her parents-in-law. Many women I spoke to hardly bothered with a Dupatta indoors while others told me in whispers that they wore it only because their mothers-in-law insisted.

The clothes people wear always have a symbolic value but for Asian women this symbolism is extremely formalised. Clothes are made with the family's approval and love but also so that women can look as their families wish to see them – modest, maternal, self-effacing, or just beautiful on their terms. In addition, clothes must help a woman to fulfil her special roles. One of these roles, given to Asian women by their families and communities, is to be the upholders and preservers of 'our culture'. So what happens if a woman wishes to have her own identity and wear clothes which she alone has chosen? All too often the loving relationships turn bitter, the easy relaxed atmosphere around the subject of clothes becomes one of anger and outrage. It is obvious that more than modesty is at stake. For example, certain materials such as denim and corduroy are considered by orthodox Muslims as unpleasant western stuff, unsuitable for women's clothing. And even outfits which are quite unrevealing can be thoroughly disapproved of. A Sikh girl from Newham, who had bought some clothes with her own money told me how her family had reacted.

The first time I wore jeans I didn't dare wear them with a sweater. So I bought a long top, which came well below my hips, to wear with them. I was really scared, the atmosphere became very stiff but nobody said anything. In the evening my mother said 'I don't like these clothes but you can do what you like. You have changed so much, you are a different person from what you used to be.'

Another reaction, just as common, was described to me by a Sikh girl from Birmingham:

I had bought a pair of trousers and a T-shirt when I had been shopping with a friend. For a long time I just could not face wearing them at home. Then one day I thought I must. I put them on in the afternoon; my mother became very silent. When my father came home all the anger seemed to burst out. He said 'You are never to wear those clothes or I'll throw you out of the house myself.'

For the girls this is only one side of the picture. On the other is the atmosphere in schools, with its contempt of anything Indian or Pakistani, which impresses on them that western dress is superior to anything Asian. For parents too (particularly for Sikh parents) there is another aspect of their lives which controls their behaviour in these circumstances. It is the position their family occupies in the hierarchy of their particular community in Britain. Families may be placed high in these hierarchies for a variety of reasons – because they have brought with them the high status they had in their villages, because they have acquired status by helping new families settle here in the fifties and sixties and kept them in a state of perennial obligation, because they have gone up in class and (as a Sikh woman in Newham told me) 'claim status by pretending to be ultra-devout and criticising others who are less so.' Families with a high status can, if they wish, be free of many traditional restrictions. They are less afraid of what the community will say. But if your family is at the bottom or middle of the community hierarchy it is under constant critical scrutiny and the women particularly have to conform (see Chapter 7). What it is like being married into a 'low status' family in the Midlands was described to me by Surjeet, a teacher in her early twenties who had grown up in Britain.

Anything western was frowned upon, so I thought I'd give it a bit of time before I got into my trousers and things. I have never worn *Chunni* over my head so I just wore it round my neck. Their mother (i.e. Surjeet's mother-in-law) kept asking me to wear it over my head. I thought after a few times she'll stop and she'll accept it. Then school started and I couldn't wear *pyamas* to school so I wore my trousers and tops . . . when they saw them they (the other wives) said 'Oh! that won't do! You'll have to wear long tops. If you are wearing trousers you'll have to wear a long top so it doesn't show anything.' But I hadn't brought anything like that with me, all my things were jumpers, so I thought – let them get used to it.
    After a few days the eldest brother told me to come. Everybody was around, everybody could hear him. He said 'In future you'll wear *pyamas* and Kamiz to school, and I have heard that you don't cover your head, though you have been asked to. When you go to school you will wear a scarf over your hair and you will be taken there every morning by your husband.' I couldn't do anything. The next day I had to wear a long Kamiz over my trousers and have a scarf covering my head – can you imagine going to school like that . . . I refused to be taken to school, but every morning before I left, the other wives would come and put make-up all over my face – bright red lipstick and things. I hate bright colours and never wear make-up but they would not listen. I used to rub it off on the way to school.

Why are certain Sikh families so keen on their women wearing make-up (in contrast to Gujerati and Muslim families where western make-up is frowned upon)? It seemed to be a sign of status. One Sikh woman in Southall told me 'My husband likes me to use make-up and I myself like it too. It is a sign of being modern and coming from a good family.' The word 'modern' used in Hindi or Punjabi does not have its English meaning, nor does it mean liberated or even progressive. Among Punjabis in Delhi who are often from the same peasant background as Punjabi immigrants to Britain a 'modern lady' is a 'respectable' urban middle-class woman. And among Punjabi peasants in Britain this Indian urban middle-class smartness, not westernisation, is the thing to aim for.

Sikhs also have a special attitude towards saris. Saris are seen as a sign of the wearer being progressive. Women from orthodox families told me that they were not allowed to wear them. One woman who wanted to wear a sari had been told by her husband 'who do you think you are – Mrs Gandhi? In future you'll stick to Salwar Kamiz as you have always done.'

Hierarchy in Asian joint families depends on age and sex but the Sikh women I spoke to all told me that in their families the disciplinarians and rulers were always men. Older women might influence decisions but they could never make them, nor could they demand obedience. (This is in striking contrast to Gujerati Hindu and Jain families where the women themselves can sometimes be tyrants over their daughters-in-law, sisters-in-law and even younger brothers-in-law, see p. 118 Chapter 7.) Sikhism is a comparatively new religion and is meant to be a religion of reform which rejects both the caste system and the oppression of women. But in practise, in India, Sikh communities have seized both these concepts and exploited them to the full. In Britain, caste is not really relevant in the same way, it usually gives rise only to petty jealousy (except where intermarriage is concerned). But the women continue to suffer a degrading subjugation. For example after their early years in Britain, Sikh women were allowed to go to work but even after all these years of earning a wage they rarely make, or are consulted about, decisions made about money. After listening to my Sikh sisters' accounts of their lives and relationships and the sensitive Izzat of their men I had the feeling that for Sikhs Izzat is not pride or honour – it is male ego, pure and simple.

But male egos differ. Muslim ones tend to shrivel up at the thought of their women going out to work. Sikh ones have learned to live with the reality of this on their own terms, while Gujerati Hindu male egos appear in general not to suffer from this particular weakness at all. A majority of Gujerati women, particularly those from East Africa, do work or look for work outside the home.

In fact, despite the links between the Hindu and Muslim ways of life in the Indian subcontinent, there is no exact analogy for Izzat among Hindus. There is reputation, one's good name and so on, but these are extensions or corollaries of Izzat rather than the thing itself. Most Gujeratis in Britain are from East Africa and have come as refugees, often with large sections of their extended family. The most important controlling factor in these families is not the male ego but hierarchy. However in Britain, with most adult members of the family earning a wage and with working life being separate from family life, hierarchy becomes a very weak concept. In India, Pakistan and East Africa the elders of a family (in-laws, husbands, older cousins, uncles and aunts) did have real power. They had economic power because they had control of the family money; and they had psychological power because the entire outside world was made up of similar families (in East Africa the Africans were socially invisible to Asians) which respected and supported the concept of hierarchy. In Britain, with more adults in the family earning their own wage, this economic power has gone. The psychological power is eroded because although the community can still disapprove of you and make you an outcast if you defy the hierarchy, beyond the community is the world of English people – an unfriendly world, but it does exist. The elders of these families – often in a pitiable condition themselves since, being old, they suffer most from being refugees – are thrown into utter confusion at their powerlessness. They respond with their age-old weapons – by trying to order their daughters-in-law about, taking away their jewellery, making their lives impossible with hundreds of petty rules, forcing sons and daughters who oppose them into arranged marriages, and, more than anything else, trying to get hold of every pay packet which is brought home. Girls of fourteen and fifteen described to me these conflicts in their own families. Sharmi told me:

It was like this – my uncle and my father came to Britain first and my uncle gave his pay packet to my father, who is older. He used to keep about half of the pay back for himself. If he wanted more he used to get it. When my grandparents came over, the next pay packet from my uncle and my father went straight to my grandfather. He would give £5 to my mum for all the cooking and £5 to my father and £5 to my uncle. When my uncle got married, they started treating my *Kaki* (aunt) badly. They would order her about like they did my mum. In the end she had a divorce because she couldn't stand it. [Divorce here means that the uncle and aunt left the grandparents' house and started living separately.] My mum stuck it out. Then my third uncle got married. In the first few weeks they treated his wife nicely. Then they took her pay packet away; they would give her only £5 and she had to go to her sisters and borrow money for her clothes and things. Then after two or three months she had had enough so she didn't give her pay packet in at all. Then the trouble really started! My grandparents really hated her. Now my uncle and aunt have moved out and so have we. We just couldn't stick it. So my grandparents live alone. It was after we left them that my father opened his own bank account.

Not all families live in this complete unit. In the family Shanta married into, the head of the family was her husband's cousin, and it was he who made the rules:

I kept my job for three months after I was married. All the money I earned in that period my husband's cousin took away from me. He gave me 50p at a time for my fares and lunch. Sometimes I had to manage on that for a week. Sometimes two weeks. Most days I'd go without food till I came home to cook the evening meal. If I asked for money from my husband he would talk of all the expenses, of how much it cost the family to keep me. I asked him why he had decided to marry me. Hadn't he realised that if he married a girl she had to eat? That cousin and his wife were against me and my husband was frightened of them. His cousin would say that I was no good, that a girl who had lost her father like me could never be any good. When I came home late after working overtime they'd say, 'she is not a good woman we must not keep her in our house.' At the same time they wanted the money which I earned. I used to work in a factory making toy guns.

These are not exceptional 'cases'. After all, most of the Gujerati women I spoke to I met through English classes they attended, through workmates and mutual friends, not through social workers and community workers. Gujerati families which live as joint families in Britain and do not have, or have never had, this strict but uneasy hierarchy must be few and far between. The women I spoke to were almost always subsidiary wage earners; the money they brought in was essential for survival but was not the main wage of the family – and their jobs were often far more unpleasant than their husband's. Many of them were sweat-shop workers, for example, while the men in their families might have white collar jobs or be shopkeepers. In most cases these families are poor, but they have brought with them the petit-bourgeois values of financially better-off days, and this has led to an apparently unquenchable materialism.

This materialism also means that the traditional tyrants, the parents-in-law, are being increasingly regarded by married couples as burdens. They have lost their power and thus their position. In some cases these old people have actually been thrown out, something unheard of in India. Where do these old people go? (More often than not they are women, since many elderly male refugees from East African have died within a few years of coming to Britain.) Their future is very bleak. The way one such woman was treated by the local services department was described in an interview with an Asian social worker (quoted from 'Some Aspects of Social Policy Affecting Asian Women in Britain' by Geeta Amin, presented at the U.K. Asian Women's Conference July 1977):

Sometimes I found the odd social worker somewhat racist or maybe so ignorant that he appeared racist. For example, there was a case of an elderly lady, Mrs X, who was living with her son and daughter-in-law. Her son had told her to leave his house. She eventually found her way to the social services department. At first the social worker appeared willing and helpful. He asked my advice and I said she should be found suitable private accommodation. Because of her isolation and loneliness Mrs X (age 68) started visiting the office every week until accommodation was arranged. Once I heard the social worker say quite seriously 'Bloody Paki – why doesn't she go home?' The same social worker eventually, quite inappropriately, arranged Part 3 accommodation for Mrs X and they placed her in a residential old people's home. Mrs X stayed there two days and came out. She didn't like it because no one spoke to her and she couldn't eat the food. The social worker complained bitterly about the fact that Mrs X had left the home, and told her off. Mrs X had no idea what she had done wrong – I eventually came to know of this situation and arranged accommodation with an Asian family.

The Gujerati community is fully aware of cases like that of Mrs X. Scandals such as hers are everybody's business, but while in India or East Africa such situations would not have been tolerated, and sons would be forced to take their mothers back, in Britain the community looks on in fascinated horror but does nothing. Perhaps people realise that in England these women are

ultimately powerless, so they feel there is no point in helping
them, or perhaps they think that the sons are to a certain extent
justified, or may be it is just a matter of people not having the time
or energy to do anything about it. Perhaps it is a sort of
demoralisation, not surprising considering the misfortunes which
have wracked the East Asian communities now in Britain
– first their years of suffering associated with their expulsion from
Africa, then their experiences at the hands of racist British
authorities who tried to keep them out of Britain, and finally the
day-to-day racism which they have faced in Britain as refugees.

They have come through it all with courage and resilience but
the community support structures have been ruptured and have
not yet been re-established – and perhaps never will be in the same
way. The women who spoke to me often had an intense nostalgia
for East Africa. 'I have known such a life . . . the days seemed to
be longer, the air sweeter than it can ever be in England . . . I had
servants who did everything. I used to be proud. We had servants.
Here it is we who are servants.' For some of them their changed
lives had brought a realisation of what their roles as women had
been in the past.

In East Africa many of us had servants – in many homes even
children were left with African 'boys'. The women had nothing to
do but flaunt their prosperity. The house was left to servants. The
ladies would visit one another, sometimes getting together to
cook delicacies in vast quantities, helping each other with the
minute tasks of the home. That was what life was like. When they
went out women would flaunt the prosperity of their families.
Here, in Britain too, some people try to do that, though for most
of us it isn't easy since we have no prosperity. Still you do see it. If
you go to Wembley on Saturday morning you will see women with
wide *Jari* bordered saris with gold embroidery, with necklaces
and bangles – all gold – and of course they don't wear a coat
because the full splendour of their clothes must be revealed – on
their feet a pair of decorative *Chappals* – however cold it might be.
They are not bothered about the weather or the customs of the
country they are in. Their personalities and identities? The
question does not arise. They are possessions and their husbands
think that is as it should be. That is how it was in East Africa, after
all. Their husbands think that it is natural for a wife to go out and
flaunt her husband's prosperity and her family's worth – that is
their tiny horizon. That happiness has some other meaning, other
sources, is not recognised.

It is true these bright galleons do sail on the high streets of Wembley on Saturday afternoons, and some will continue to do so for many years to come – but not all. Those who will continue to do so will be there of their own free will as status bearers of the nuclear family, a role common enough among English women, but not as possessions. Because that role is finished now for East African women. They have begun a new life as workers.

As for the Gujerati joint family it looks as though nothing can save it now. When nuclear family segments break off from the joint family for one reason or another, the values of the joint family nevertheless continue to plague them. The maintaining of the male ego in perfect condition remains an essential activity of the nuclear family. For example when, as a journalist, I visited couples in their homes to ask about local events, my conversations with women would often be interrupted by their husbands holding up their hands in the direction of their wives and saying in the most matter of fact way 'Be quiet,' and then turning to me and saying 'There is no point in asking my wife. She does not know. She is not educated.' In most cases these wives were literate and well informed, but they would smile politely and agree with their husbands. When I spoke to some of these women alone much later I asked them why Asian women often reacted like this; their answers were that it was good for a man's Izzat. At the same time the wife's role was to serve, and this modest withdrawal was as it were a part of the service.

Even in the nuclear family, women told me that certain jobs should never be done by a man, they were not Izzat *wali kam* (i.e. jobs of honour) or they were not manly, and predictably these tasks included almost all household chores. The question of a couple being happy or unhappy did not really seem to arise. But a marriage could be smooth and peaceful, and many were, as long as the man carried out his duties towards his wife and a woman was submissive to her husband. As a Muslim woman from Jhelum explained to me, in Islam a man can marry four times but according to Islam it is his duty to look after each of his wives and treat them honourably. 'My husband has married only once,' she told me 'but he has forgotten that he has any duties.' An East African Asian Hindu women told me about a man's responsibilities (her husband was carrying them out very successfully, she said) 'I think it is a man's fault if his wife is backward. It is a man's responsibility to educate himself but also to educate his wife and children.'

Only a few women were on equal terms with their husbands and they recognised their relationships as exceptional. One of them, a Sikh woman in her late forties, encouraged me to write about those duties which a husband should fulfil. 'It is up to a man,' she said 'to make a marriage a source of peace or misery, because the man has power; our women usually have none.' Of her own marriage she said 'Sometimes I forget that we are husband and wife. We can say anything to each other. We are so close so equal. We seem just like two friends.'

III
Work Outside the Home
'Next time I won't cry, I'll make you cry'

We had a shop in Nairobi and came here when we got our vouchers in 1971. After coming here I worked for four months in a sweet factory in Stratford. The work was very hard and we were paid only £13 a week. We had to make a ring out of peanut dough. You were paid depending on how many trayfuls you were able to make, 24 or 28. But I could never really make enough. One day I had an argument with the forelady. She said 'You must work faster or it won't do!' I said 'These hands I have got, they are hands not a machine!' Then she said 'I won't have you answering back, you will be given your cards, you'll be sacked.' I said 'O.K., I can only work as much as I can physically, no more.' So she said 'We'll throw you out.' After that for some months I was unemployed. Then I got a job in a laundry.

Asian women are the worst off of all British workers. They are at the bottom of the heap. They come unprepared, easy victims to unscrupulous employers. They don't know the language so their choice of jobs is limited to the worst and least skilled; they don't know their rights so they can be intimidated, they don't have much information about other, better off workers so they can be paid poverty-line wages. They are black so they need not be treated even like women, but more like animals. And if they ever ask for help against their employers, their chances of getting it are usually (despite Grunwick, see later in this chapter) known to be small. Neither their husbands and families, nor white trade unionists nor middle-class Asians are keen to help them.

For middle-class Asians their working-class sisters do not really exist. At a recent meeting of middle-class Asian women gathered to organise a conference of Asian women in Britain, I mentioned the word working-class. 'What does it mean?' one of these exquisitely saried ladies asked with a slight transatlantic drawl, 'surely in this day and age we all work. We don't live on unearned income or own stocks and shares.' Several others agreed with her. Among Indians and Pakistanis, they told me rather severely, there is no class system as there is among English people. One tentative voice asked if I meant 'deprived women like those of the East End', but this too was slapped down by others – 'in these days of inflation, aren't we all deprived?'

After visiting the cool, elegant (suburban) drawing rooms of rich Asians one might wonder just how these women are materially deprived. They may, as in the case of Mrs H——, have an Asian woman servant to do 'all the kitchen work, cleaning the pantry, fridge, floors and preparing all the *Nashta* and everything.' In the last ten years, Mrs H. tells me, she has always had a servant, because without one, social duties, cooking, and housework, even with the most up-to-date equipment, proved too exhausting.

For the house (cleaning) I have somebody else. Formerly I had an English couple who used to come every day, that lasted seven or eight years then they got too old. Now I have a girl who comes from – Indonesia? No, Philippines, that's it! She has two days off from her family where she's working, so she comes those two days. Now my children are grown up so I don't need constant help.

The proportion of Asian women in Britain who are as well-off as Mrs H. is minute, but they are often the ones who are prominent on race-relations bodies and community relations sub-committees. It is they who hold dialogue with establishment spokesmen, sitting side by side with white experts and a few Asian men on the 'problems' and 'needs' of Asian women. They rarely cross the paths of working-class Asians except in the course of their occasional investigations. Their lives are rarely laid side by side for comparison with those of working women – women like Shahida or Prabhaben (Chapter 7) who work all day in laundries, component factories and sweat-shops 'till my feet are like bricks and my arms aching . . . at night it used to be agony till I fell asleep.' In the brief moments of respite they get they sometimes wonder, like Champaben, a homeworker;

Is this what life is for, is this why my parents brought me up with so much love and care? Ask them if they are working-class or middle-class, and they tell you 'This is our fate, sister, to work, to slave, in Pakistan too some of us had to do the hard, hard work on the fields. Here it is a different kind of work, we are more lonely and in some ways the work is harder, but for us women as you

know, life itself is very hard . . . Yes, maybe there are some
women who don't have to work, their husbands are well off and
love them, but they often stay indoors all day and that is not nice.
Women with servants in Britain? Really? Are there such women?
It must be so since you say. I have never seen them.

For Asian women wage labour is a new experience, both baffling
and exciting. Baffling because it is all so new and strange, and
exciting because it brings the first hint, the first distant suggestion
that for women an independent economic identity is possible.
Asian women who are wage earners fall into three main groups –
homeworkers, shop assistants and secretaries, and factory and
sweat-shop workers. In this chapter I shall write only about
women in the last group and their position in the British labour
market since very little has been written about them.

Before they came to Britain, Asian women from a peasant
background were agricultural workers doing as much work on
the land as men did. But they did not earn a separate wage, they
lived in effect in a mainly cashless society. This society seemed self-
contained; those who felt exploited could easily identify the
enemy – the landlord or money lender. Whatever organisation
was possible at village level was usually directed against him. The
idea of comparing wages did not arise because (in the small
holdings of Punjab, for example) the question of wages hardly
ever arose. When people from this background find themselves in
the middle of an industrial set-up, it is not easy for them to adjust
their values or frames of reference, just as people from an
industrial society, used to individual wages and jobs, would feel
confused if suddenly thrust into a peasant society.

Surinder, a Sikh woman, explained to me what it had been like
coming to Britain in the sixties and finding a job in a sweat-shop
soon after.

It used to be amazing at the end of the week to be paid, to have
money in your hand for the work you had done. It was very little
money really, but to me in those days it seemed like a lot. Money
in this society means quite different things and that really hit me.
At home, money meant food or perhaps, if one had saved a lot,
more land, but here the shops were full of the most amazing
commodities and getting money at the end of the week seemed to
suggest that these things were within one's reach. For a long time I
never realised how badly paid and overworked I was, but what
made me feel bad in those days was the rudeness and lack of

respect with which I and other Asian women were treated by the supervisors. Now I have begun to understand, bad pay, rotten conditions and this insufferable contempt shown to us, it is a part of the same picture.

What makes this understanding, this adjustment even more difficult are the immense problems of everyday life in Britain – how to get to work, how to sign your name and so on. But once these hurdles are overcome, women soon stop harking back to their village background and comparing everything with it. The next stage is when they begin to think of themselves as workers in Britain and compare their lives with those of other workers, black and white. More and more women from a peasant background are now reaching this stage – a fact which can't be ignored by employers. The 'docile', easily exploited workforce is gradually becoming more defiant and angry. As a personnel manager in a Bradford mill put it 'Asian ladies are so well behaved. They have no complaints, they complete their training period very accurately and they are really good. We are very happy to have them. But lately these ladies in the Spinning department, they seem to be rather odd. They can be rude. It concerns me because it is unusual for an Asian lady to be rude, to answer back, to be a chatter-box.'

If that is the case with ex-peasants, these 'reactions from experience' for women from an urban background, say from Kenya, are different. They have never worked before outside their home or family shop but the concepts of a commercial society are quite familiar to them. Those of them from East Africa were, before they came here, middle-class or lower middle-class. Because of this, their expectations are often higher. They know nothing about the means of organising, nor are they particularly militant, but they see quickly and quite clearly that they are being exploited.

Prabhaben, a woman in her thirties, described to me the conditions at the laundry where she works. (For the full interview with Prabhaben, see Chapter 7, 'Sisters in Struggle'.) Of about 50 employees, 40 are Asian women.

You ask about discrimination? There is a colour bar, that is for certain. First the pay; Indians get less. Oh yes, the whites get more. We get £28 a week whether we are sitting at a machine all day or operating heavy presses. The white women get £32. Upstairs where the machines are it is terribly hot. It is very difficult to work there. Almost all the workers upstairs are women, there are only two men and they are pensioners. The women's salary is very low. The pay in laundries is very poor, they can't afford to pay more, that is what they say. In many ways I am better off than the others, I work downstairs. Upstairs the women suffer, they really suffer. They are paid low salaries and everything is worse for them, they have to face the insults of supervisors. These supervisors are all English women.

The trouble is that in Britain our women are expected to behave like servants, and we are not used to behaving like servants and we can't. But if we behave normally like saying a few words to each other, the supervisors start shouting and harrassing us. Or if they go to the toilet and take just a little longer. Of course white women do that too but the supervisors don't notice them. They complain about us Indians to the manager. Our women suffer so much, but usually they don't come out and complain. They don't know English but it is more than that. It is that all your life you have been soft and this treatment shocks and stuns you. But one or two of us have begun to speak up. Veena who lives in Manor House, she is good. She doesn't take any rubbish and there are one or two others like her.

At Prabhaben's laundry there is no union. That is the norm in the small workplaces which employ Asian women. Conditions in these places are often not only uncomfortable but unsafe. The factory inspectorate has never heard of their existence. These work-places belong to two main types of firms – largish firms in traditionally low wage industries such as laundries or electrical component factories or sweet factories, or sweat-shops – where the employer may be a family firm or a self-made man, fiercely anti-union, determined to compete with bigger firms if necessary, by exploiting his workers. As far as personalities are concerned, the second type of employer is frequently the sort of man who forms the backbone of the ultra-right in Britain and is usually a racist in the most extreme and overt sense. The work offered is often seasonal, like making Christmas decorations or making and packing anything from toy guns to cheap electric heaters. The attitude to the Asian women employed is that they should be hired and fired as needed.

Before Asian women began working in large numbers, their jobs were done by Asian men or white women. Even now, many factories employ varying proportions of these two other groups alongside Asian women, but a white man would almost never work in such a place except as a supervisor.

Spiralynx (1933) is a bedding factory in East London. The factory, in Russell Road, Canning Town, was acquired in the 1940s by Montague Goodman, the managing director of MG Furniture Reproductions Ltd, a small factory in South Hackney. He also acquired factories in Hanbury Street and Rowland Street, E1, and obtained the patent for manufacturing spiral linked mattresses. In the 1950s and 60s he took over or formed a number of firms – Sun Resta Ltd, Multi Resta Ltd, Sleepy Valley Ltd etc, and one, Multi Spring Ltd in Mitcham Surrey, which according to its headed note paper are 'contractors to HM Government'. Government bodies and local authorities are prohibited by legislation from dealing with companies paying below the agreed minimum wage. But the existence of a group where the products from one factory may be marketed in another allows for the possibility of products being internally sold.

Between 1968 and 1970 the factories from Hanbury Street and Rowland Street were transferred to Russell Road, Canning Town. By 1975 80% of the workforce were Asian and 15% were women. The conditions inside the factory were described in a report by the Newham Careers Office made on 17 October 1975:

I can only say I was shocked and disgusted by the conditions in the factory, which were seen to constitute definite health and safety hazards. All the machines were archaic with no proper safeguards, e.g. guillotines, spring-making machines and other similar machines with a cutting edge had no automatic stopping device. In the metal and spring-making department the floor was littered with pieces of metal, coils of wire and shavings; the surface of the floor was greasy and the premises generally filthy. The machines in the spring department gave off choking fumes and a grey pall seemed to hang over the department . . . about 90 per cent of the work force are coloured, many of whom cannot speak English. I counted only six white workers in the factory, half of which seemed to be of below average intelligence. The total work force equals 150, it was noted that the workers all looked rather miserable and depressed and the working atmosphere was not at all pleasant. I was not allowed to speak to the workers . . . it seems that their trade union membership is not allowed by the management.

What kind of people constitute the management of Spiralynx? David Goodman, son of Monty and also a director, gave this account in an interview (conducted by the staff of Canning Town

Community Development Project) in January 1975. 'I am talking of people of our calibre; two or three men, a couple of hundred staff, good solid firms that normally don't go bankrupt . . . They live out their business lives well, never become millionaires but they are solid citizens.'

Since 1964 the Furniture unions have tried three times to organise the workers of Spiralynx; each time a small number of workers have joined a union, the management have found out and workers have been dissuaded from joining. In the last attempt, in 1975, what made unionisation especially difficult was that, although most of the workers were then Asians, they spoke different languages. The workforce was in fact exceptionally fragmented. These attempts at unionisation failed completely.

In fact the main lessons of these attempts seems to be to those outside Spiralynx – that organising from the outside is impossible. Workers in a place like Spiralynx can only be organised if there is an explosion of anger and discontent inside the factory strong enough for a large number of workers to take a stand, at the risk of losing their own jobs. It is only after this that the supporting role of outside sympathisers can be useful. The attitude of outside well-wishers has too often been like that of a left-wing friend of mine who asked in the early days of the Grunwick strike 'Who is doing the organising there?' – as though the workers were just so much raw material waiting to be organised.

No one, least of all Asian women workers themselves, would claim that they are highly militant or strong. What they have been in the past, in the face of their grim working lives, is resilient. They have refused to despair, accepting quite stoically what they have been given. Now this stoicism is changing. Partly it is changing because women are getting more familiar with the industrial scene and partly because of the tremendous impact and influence of the strike at Grunwick Photoprocessing. That strike has proved for always that Asian women workers can be strong, resourceful and courageous, that they can stand up, face the world and demand their rights.

In Britain there has for many years been a sub-proletariat, a sub-class of the working class who are far worse off than the main body, consisting of sweat-shop workers and homeworkers, people who are treated by employers as though they have no rights at all. Before Asian immigrants came to Britain, these jobs were done by previous waves of immigrants in certain areas (like the East End of London). But elsewhere in the country in general they were usually done by indigenous working-class women whose mothers had often had similar jobs before them. Now that Asian women have taken over their positions, they move upwards, even though only slightly upwards, in the labour hierarchy. But this means more than just one group replacing another. The change is a tremendous one. At the bottom of the hierarchy of the production structure, where spirits are assumed to be crushed, have come a new army of workers – fresh, vivacious and increasingly angry. Their expectations are high because many of them have, until recently, had a middle-class life and outlook (ie. the East African Asians) and because, unlike the British working class, they have not been ground down and prepared for their jobs by the British education system. Apart from this, their race, and often their language, gives them a solidarity which white workers can only rarely achieve. If they win their battles, as one trade union organiser put it (while describing Grunwick) 'it will be a new dimension in trade union activity'. In other words it would mean that battles could be won which people have previously thought could not even be fought.

At this lowest level of British industry it is almost as though struggles are not expected to occur, let alone be won. Trade unions, if they are involved at all, are not meant to be militant. This is because of the structure of trade unions themselves in Britain. They are a concession, a compromise between workers and employers and an accepted unit in the capitalist structure. Not surprisingly, the unions or union branches of the most powerful workers (ie. those who have the greatest effect on capital) are in general the strongest. The unions or union branches organising workers less crucial to capital are weaker, till at the lowest stage of trade union structure the union becomes just a formality. It is never expected to take up demands or make a real effort to change conditions. In fact it often acts just as a damper, the first hurdle workers have to overcome. (Dozens of of strikes of black workers illustrate this; for details see issues of the magazine *Race Today*.)

It isn't often that unions have taken up issues such as racial or sex discrimination or unfair dismissal, and when workers have come out on strike they have usually been slow and reluctant to make these strikes official. But while union hierarchy is crucial in the amount of support workers get, it is counterbalanced by another important factor, the political complexion of the union branch at local level. Take the cases of two well-known strikes involving women – the strikes at Trico and at Electrolux. The first received full support of the trade union, the second did not. The reason was that at Trico the district committee (which in the engineering union structure is a very important body) was dominated by the left while at Electrolux it was controlled by the right. Obviously the same is true on the question of racism. Branches dominated by the left are less likely to be racialist, but unfortunately in many areas with large immigrant populations, like Leicester and Loughborough, the important union bureaucracies are controlled by the right wing. In these areas, for black workers, conventional industrial struggles must be preceded by a battle with the racists in the trade union. That is what happened at both Imperial Typewriters in Leicester and at Mansfield Hosiery in Loughborough.

Imperial Typewriters was a large firm, but again, like Grunwick, Spiralynx and so many others, marginal to British capital. Conditions there were the sort with which Asian women everywhere in Britain are familiar. Two aspects were described by women workers interviewed in *Race Today*:

I assemble motors in the store department. When I first started work here I had to make 14 motors per hour. But then they raised the target to 16 then to 18 and so on. Now it is 22. To work at that speed we can't even drink a cup of tea. We have no official tea break but sometimes one of us goes out and gets tea for the others. But then if the foreman sees, he starts complaining about us in front of all the other workers, and even the supervisor, saying we always waste time and talk too much. Anyway, we didn't complain about that. We complained to them about the target. We all said 22 is too high. However hard we work we can never make more than that – and unless we make more we don't get any bonus. But on top of that if we make less than 22, say 20 or 21, they cut some money from our basic pay . . . We are mostly Asians in our section, but our shop steward is a white woman. She doesn't care and the union doesn't care. I pay 11p a week to be a member of the union but I really think it is a waste of hard earned money. Don't get me wrong. I am not against unions but our union is no different from management.

I went to our shop steward one day and explained that the 22 target was too high. I also told her that the supervisor had asked us to oil our own machines that morning. Normally our machines are oiled before we come in. I told her that oiling was not our job and that management was always trying to make us do more work for the same pay. She told me not to make a fuss over such a small thing. That is the kind of shop steward she is. This is why we must have our own shop stewards. In this factory there are 1100 of us and yet we only have one Asian shop steward. It doesn't make sense, does it? . . . this way we are not represented at all.

Finally on 1 May 1974, while other workers in Leicester were demonstrating their militancy with May Day strikes, 39 Asian workers walked out of section 61 at Imperial Typewriters. Of these 39, 27 were women. They had worked at assembling parts into complete typewriters. The women were being paid £18 a week on piece work, the men £25. In addition they were supposed to receive bonus rates after the daily target of 200 machines a day. The company policy had been to speed up the line and the rate of production. The workers in section 61 were angry because they felt, firstly, that the quotas of production allocated to white workers were unfair compared with the quota allocated to them; secondly, because conditions of work were different for Asian workers – their washing times, lunch breaks and toilet breaks were restricted; and thirdly because, although most of the workers were Asians, the union branch had an overwhelmingly white shop steward's committee (there was only one Asian shop steward) which was not only uninterested in their struggles but actively opposed to them.

In the course of their demands to Reg Weaver, the T&GWU factory convenor, the workers from section 61 found out that although they were being paid bonuses on a target of 200 or more they were in fact entitled to bonuses on 168 (an agreement which dated back to 1972 and would have meant £4 a week extra). Within 2 days, 500 more workers joined the 39 people from section 61. They demanded an end to the use of racism by management to divide workers. They called for democratic elections in the trade unions. They stood by their demands for back-dated bonus payments. The company's response was to issue notice to the original 40 that if they didn't return to work they'd all be sacked. In this period the trade union branch's attitude is best expressed by the trade union negotiator himself – George Bromley JP. 'The workers have not followed the proper dispute procedures, they have no legitimate grievances and it is difficult to know what they want.' Later Bromley spoke to Radio Leicester about the management at Imperial Typewriters, Asian women and race generally:

The Imperial management, they are not American-style management at all. I've no brief for management and by and large I don't find many managements very efficient, but I'll say this,

Imperial Typewriter management are soft and if we have got a case we have no difficulty in winning it, no difficulty . . . Let us take the question of the ladies' toilets which you asked me about. Now this is a reputable firm there are plenty of Factory Acts. No company stops people going to the toilet. This is so ludicrous it is laughable in modern times.

What happens here is that if a white lady wants to go to the toilet and she's working on a line, she doesn't ask anyone's permission, she just gets up – out she goes, powders her nose, has a cigarette, whatever they do – then comes back. Nobody bothers. Back on the line she goes and work continues. Now some of these Asian ladies, I feel sorry for them, they are strangers, they don't know much about industrial life, they have led a very sheltered life, you know, and when they go to the toilet they go together. If there are 38 of them on the line, 38 go together for ten minutes and then, of course, the line stops. That's when the foreman begins to go in to hook them out. It's not that he wants to stop them going to the toilet, we've got to persuade these people to do it on a stagger basis . . . I feel sorry for people that are dumped into a civilisation such as ours and they are taking the sticky end of the stick in these low-rated factories. Because they are semi-skilled they are low rated but they have got to learn to fit in with our ways you know. We haven't got to fit in with theirs. And the way they have been acting, that means they will close factories and people won't employ them – that's all.

The Imperial Typewriters strike was seen by many people as a defeat. The strikers returned to work having won few concessions. But for the women involved it was also a kind of victory. One of them, Shardha Behn, described her feelings in an interview just after the strike (*Race Today*, Sept 1974):

The first day I got back to work, my foreman asked me what I had gained in the last twelve weeks. He was making fun of me I know. But I told him that I had lost a lot of money but had gained a lot of things. I told him I had learnt how to fight against him for a start. I told him he couldn't push me around any more like a football from one job to another. I told him I now knew many things I didn't know before. In the past when I used to get less money in my wage packet I used to start crying at once. I didn't know what else to do. I told the foreman, 'Next time I won't cry, I'll make you cry.'

The strike at Imperial Typewriters demonstrated clearly the conflict between the trade union bureaucracy and black workers.

Three years later the TUC attitude to black workers, and more specifically black women workers, was shown by its lack of action on such simple and bland recommendations (from the Camden Council for Community Relations) as that the trade union movement should press for compulsory language training at work (ie. in the employer's time, not after hours) or co-operate 'more positively' in agreeing to English classes where the management has taken the initiative, or that there should be 'more positive participation in supporting any industrial action taken by minority group workers in their fight to achieve equal opportunity'. As a *Race Today* editorial (in October 1974) put it, 'the section to benefit most from the trade unions are white men over the age of thirty-five. Nowhere is this as clearly illustrated as in the struggles of black workers and in the way in which white workers have aligned themselves with the bureaucracy.' That is still true in 1978. In fact, in many factories all over Britain white workers are not only on the side of trade union bureaucracy but often on the side of the management against their black workmates. But there has been an important exception. In the most important strike of 1976 and 1977 the rank and file of the labour movement have demonstrated their support of black workers.

The strike at Grunwick Photoprocessing is exceptional in many ways. Not only are the men and women involved people of remarkable courage and strength, but unlike Imperial Typewriters or Spiralynx it is a strike of black workers in an area well known for its tradition of left wing trade union organisation. Jack Dromey of Brent Trades Council told me:

Willesden and Stonebridge (in NW London) used to be known in the 30s as Red Willesden and Red Stonebridge. They have a long tradition of solid trade union organisation. Industrially the area is dominated by light engineering and manufacturing in the major industrial estates of Park Royal, part of East Acton, Wembley trading estate, East Lane Wembley and a number of independent factories scattered throughout the borough. Outside of Dagenham and East London, the home of Fords, it is the biggest centre of industry left in London. A number of the large employers have gone over the last ten or fifteen years but there are still very large industrial complexes. For example, in Park Royal you get traditional strongholds of trade union movement like Park Royal vehicles, which, together with AECs in Southall, is the centre of bus building for British Leyland. Also Brent East has

the highest concentration of immigrants of any parliamentary
constituency in the country. Not only black immigrants but Irish
immigrants as well. You get a number of convenors and shop
stewards who are Asian, West Indian or Irish. It is unlike East
London, where over the last ten or twenty years the heart has been
torn out of manufacturing industry in the docks and with it has
gone traditional working-class organisation.

However, even in this atmosphere of working-class confidence
there are a number of factories and work-places where working
conditions are utterly degrading. Grunwick Photoprocessing
could be any factory employing Asians in any part of Britain. It is
not in the mainstream of capitalist enterprise, Kodak or Agfa
could easily do without it, in fact if it closed down the person
worst off would be its director George Ward. In 1973-74 the firm
made a profit of £126,719 after tax; the workers were then being
paid £28 for a 40-hour week. In August 1976, when the strike
started, their pay had not changed. In 1976, 80 per cent of the 440
workers were Asians, in fact it seemed that management
deliberately set out to employ Asians since employment application forms asked for passport numbers and dates of arrival in the
UK. Jayaben Desai, perhaps Britain's best known Asian trade
unionist, described to me in the early days of the strike what it had
been like working at Grunwick:

At the Dollis Hill factory the conditions were the same as
elsewhere in Grunwick, the aim was to employ our people and
from them to take as much as possible, for as little as possible. At
Dollis Hill they had developed their own system. On two sides
there are glass cabins for the management so that they can watch
you from both sides. And the supervisor or foreman can watch
you as well. He is English. He moves around and keeps an eye.
You have to put up your hand and ask even to go to the toilet. If
someone is sick, say a woman has a period or something, they
wouldn't allow her home without a doctor's certificate, and if
someone's child was sick and they had to take it to the clinic or
hospital they would say 'Why are you going, ask someone else
from your family to go.' Perhaps they thought that having a day
off would be a chance of getting another job and breaking their
hold on us.
      Even pregnant women who wanted to go to the clinic were told
'You must arrange to go at the weekend.' On the rare occasions
when a woman did go during working hours she would be warned

that that was the last time. Everyone would be paid a different wage so no one knew what anyone else was getting. And to force people to work they would make them fill in a job sheet saying how many films they had booked in. If someone did a large number they would bring the job sheet around and show the others and say 'She has done so many, you also must.' Not that they were paid more!

Of course the young girls, they sometimes started off very enthusiastic and perhaps did do quite a lot without realising the implications and effects of it. But the older women often had trouble keeping up. The system was forever escalating; say someone did 300, it is not as though you could try and make 300 and feel you were getting on all right, because next month someone might do 400 and then you would be pushed and bullied to try and increase your pace further. The older women found it a terrible strain. I used to tell my husband about all these harassments, he is a union member, and he was aware of all the advantages of belonging to a union. But somehow for a long time it never occurred to me how to get it all started, how it was possible.

Then my job was at one stage to clear payments and complaints. In the evening when the booking and despatch department would start packing up to go, so would I and no one asked me not to. Then one day the foreman came and said 'Mrs Desai, why have you packed up?' I said 'Why not?' There was work left over, it is true, but there often was. There was often just too much for me to finish on my own. The foreman said 'Who asked you to pack up?' I said 'No one ever asks me.' He couldn't answer, but the second-in-command at the place appeared and said 'Mrs Desai, I have some work for you.' I said 'I know that, you have your work but I have my work too. I want to know what all the fuss is about. Nobody has told me before to pack up, why are you bringing it up today?' He had no answer, but in the meantime the manager appeared and asked me to come into the office.

I thought that I would go in and explain the whole thing to him and explain that there was no point in creating trouble un-necessarily. But before I could say anything he started to shout at me, saying 'Mrs Desai, you can't talk back to me or to Mr Diffy or Mr Mike.' I said 'I am here to tell you something but if you don't want to listen to me I am not going to listen to you either.' He said 'Mrs Desai, don't point at me.' I said 'If you point at me I can point at you.' He said 'I warn you.' I said 'I don't want your warning. I am going to leave this job. I have worked loyally, shown you respect, but I too expect to be treated with respect. You bring me into the office to shout at me and I can't say anything. I just have to listen, I am not going to stand this.'

I went out where the rest of the staff were working and I told them 'I am leaving. You all know very well what the management are doing. This has happened to me today, it will happen to you tomorrow. You have to wake up.' Why aren't they employing white people in this factory. Because the white workers would teach them how to treat them. We are not teaching them, that is why they are treating us like this. I told the manager, 'You misjudge people, you think they are daft. But they are not. Some have problems, some because of their circumstances are working here. But I am not like that. You can't treat me like that. I will prove it to you.' I walked out and my son Sunil was behind me – he walked out too.

That afternoon they had already sacked one boy and four others had walked out in support. I didn't know much about it. But when I walked out I saw them standing outside. They were thinking of doing some violence, they were so angry. I saw them standing in a crowd; they told me 'We want to prove something, show them something.' I said 'You can't prove anything by violence. You need a concrete plan. Otherwise you'll just hurt yourself and end up in jail. Nothing will change.' I suggested forming a union.

They asked me, how? I said I didn't know either but between us all we could find out. We all agreed on that.

It was Friday, 20 August 1976. On Monday we arrived at the factory with placards we had made demanding a union. We thought, specially the boys, that placards and a demonstration were important. We stood outside the factory and asked workers entering to sign a petition demanding a union. Then we went to the Citizen's Advice Bureau (CAB) at Wembley, as my husband had suggested, and asked them for information about how to join a union. It was soon after that that we contacted APEX and the Willesden Law Centre, and got in touch with Jack Dromey.

At that stage, says Jack Dromey, the law centre's representative on the Strike Committee.

They were as green as grass, they were like a bunch of lost chickens outside the coop. They were so green that they were going to the CAB to find out about unions. Now to be honest if they had come to us first we would have got them into another union the T&GWU or ACTT but having said that, one thing we should knock on the head straight away. Some people have said that if they joined the T&G or ACTT the strike would have been over much quicker. I don't believe it. I don't believe that with any union this company would have been cracked any quicker. Anyway, they were in contact with APEX and then they came to see us, that was on a Monday, the same day there were mass meetings at Chapter Road and Cobbold Road. On Tuesday they all got together in the Trades and Labour Hall and they were very excited at that stage. There was a tremendous release of tension, particularly for the people, the women who had been permanent workers as opposed to the students, they had been through the most appalling experiences, the most utter degradation. It was a tremendous relief for them to get out of the company and take a stand in the way they had done.

But taking this stand was not easy, particularly for the women. There were at Grunwick a group of exceptional women, women of great dignity and strength of personality like Jayaben Desai and Kalaben Patel who although in no sense 'westernised' had rejected traditional attitudes that women should be submissive and passive. It was they who formed the core of the strikers, persuading and supporting other weaker women. They visited the homes of these women, talked to husbands, fathers and fathers-in-law who did not want them to take part in any struggle, and they urged the women themselves to assert themselves. This was a tremendous task because, as Jayaben Desai told me:

Our Gujerati women are often weak, weakened by the acceptance that their life must revolve round dressing up, housework, wearing jewellery and other things like that. Often it does not occur to them that they can speak up, raise their voices in front of people. Personally I don't think it is traditions which are weighing them down but the fact that they have no support at home. Their husbands don't want them to do anything which is not passive, and in the end women end up believing the same. In my case, for example, my husband gives me every help. If I can't read or understand something in the paper he discusses it with me – about what is happening in the country or the community or about what politics can mean. Few husbands treat their wives like that.

All too often husbands actually prevented their wives from coming to the picket line and there were cases where parents-in-law forced women to go on working for the sort of reasons described in Chapter 6. Apart from the purely oppressive aspect – that these people felt that women must be seen and not heard, that taking part in an industrial struggle was not right for a woman – there was the undeniable fact that in these families money was desperately needed. Most of them were refugees from East Africa living in substandard conditions and paying exorbitant rents; for them a second income was desperately needed, and going on strike seemed a dangerous business.

The management at Grunwick had always made use of the poverty of Asians: they had preferred them to English workers to the extent that white women applying for jobs there would actually be turned away. As the Grunwick men and women frequently commented 'Imagine how humiliating it was for us, particularly for older women, to be working and to overhear the employer saying to a young English girl "you don't want to come and work here, love, we won't be able to pay the sort of wages that'll keep you here" – while we had to work there because we were trapped.' But the directors of the company were also aware of the position of Asian women in their community and they tried to use it when they came out on strike. George Ward, the owner of Grunwick, is an Anglo-Indian. Jayaben said:

He would come to the picket line and try to mock us and insult us. One day he said 'Mrs Desai, you can't win in a sari, I want to see you in a mini'. I said 'Mrs Gandhi she wears a sari and she is ruling a vast country.' I spat at him 'I have my husband behind me and I'll wear what he wants me to.' He was very angry and he started referring to me as big mouth. On my second encounter with Ward he said 'Mrs Desai, I'll tell the whole Patel community that you are a loose woman.' I said 'I am here with this placard! Look! I am showing all England that you are a bad man. You are going to tell only the Patel community but I am going to tell all of England.' Then he realised that I would not weaken and he tried to get at the younger girls. About one girl he started spreading the story that she had come out only to join her boyfriend. He did this because he knew that if it got to her parents they would force her to go back in. You see he knows about Indian society and he is using it. Even for those inside he has found for each one an individual weakness, to frighten some and to shame others. He knows that Indian women are often easily shamed.

But the women were changing as well. As Mahmood, the secretary of the strike committee, put it in the tenth month of the strike 'When the women first joined Grunwick they were just like ordinary Indian women. But now many of them can stand up in front of the gate and talk back to the managing director. If he swears, swear back at him. They can face it, which they wouldn't do before.' They had come a long way from a meeting in the very early days when Sunil Desai, Jayaben's son and then secretary of the strike committee, had suggested that the men do the picketing and women make the tea. But according to both Jayaben and Jack Dromey, it was established from that very meeting onwards that the women must play an equal role. Every delegation sent out by the strikers to talk to workers at other factories consisted of two men and two women.

I asked Mahmood whether he thought the attitude of the male strikers towards the woman had changed at all. He said 'Not all of them have changed. Some of the people who are more involved, like myself, have realised that women are playing as important a role as the men. But on the whole I don't think that most of the men have changed their ideas or attitude that much.' Did they feel that women couldn't be militant? 'No, it is not that, they can see that women are more militant than the men, doing more work on the picket line. But as far as their ideas of women in society goes it hasn't changed – that women should stay home and do the cooking.' Why was it, I asked Mahmood, that although a majority of workers at Grunwick were women the strike committee consisted (till then) mainly of men? His answer was:

The only reason is that we are younger and we have more freedom, we can do what we like. At 2 or 3 hours notice we may have to go to Manchester; the women can't do that. We could go up there and be there a week. The women can't do that, those who are married because they are married and those who are not married because they are not married. Though if you give them enough notice they can do almost anything . . . In their personal freedom I wouldn't say they are free like English girls but they are up to a point. When the strike started they were completely different.

Since as Jack Dromey put it, Brent, with its left-wing trade unionists, 'was a bloody good place for the Grunwick strike to happen', one might expect that the union involved had given the strikers not only support but increased impetus in their struggles, but members of the strike committee certainly did not feel this to be so. Mahmood told me (at the end of May 1977):

As far as APEX is concerned they are OK up to a point but they just want to follow the legal procedures and we want them to take some kind of militant action. At the start we asked them to approach the Union of Post Office Workers (UPW) to cut off the mail to Grunwick but they wouldn't do that either. They were always very slow in responding. They always want to follow legal procedures up to a point, when even they realised that without some kind of help from other unions they were not going to win this strike. We had to push them all the time, all the time.

The legal procedures APEX had suggested consisted of approaching the government conciliation body ACAS (Advisory, Conciliation and Arbitration Service) which operates within the Employment Protection Act and was a part of the Social Contract. It was the Grunwick dispute which was to show conclusively the ineffectiveness of ACAS, hailed till then as 'a concession to the workers'. The activities of ACAS were as follows: On 31 August 1976 they approached the Grunwick management to start conciliation and were immediately rebuffed. On the 4th November the management, by then under pressure (for reasons unconnected with APEX or ACAS) agreed that ACAS should ballot the workers on whether they wanted union recognition. On 26 November Grunwick again refused to cooperate with ACAS if sacked workers were balloted. On 20 December ACAS decided to go ahead with the balloting, though Grunwick refused to supply the names and addresses of those working. On 2 February ACAS published a draft report and finally in March 1977, six months after they first came on the scene, they published the full report on Grunwick recommending recognition of APEX. That was the end of the ACAS story because Grunwick flatly and legally refused to accept its recommendations.

In June 1977 the Strike Committee had finally had enough of these bureaucratic manipulations forced on them by APEX. They decided to call upon the support of the rank and file of the labour movement. A week of action began on 13 June with a mass picket, at which 84 people were arrested and there was large scale police violence. In the next few weeks the size of the picket increased, reaching 2,500 on 23 June. Police injuries, 243 in August 1977 (according to Merlyn Rees, Home Secretary), continually made headlines but in fact about three times as many pickets were injured. According to a Willesden doctor quoted in *Time Out* (August 12-18) 'Two types of injury are particularly common: the first is a result of testicles being grabbed by the police. The second is a result of women having their breasts grabbed.' These injuries went in general unreported in the media. For example, BBC Television on the evening of the 11 July Day of Action, and the papers next morning, were full of pictures of injured policemen, but the pickets who were injured were hardly mentioned, although among them was a man who had had an epileptic fit, a woman who had collapsed at the rear entrance to the factory and two Yorkshire miners who had to be carried away by their friends.

Not only was there overwhelming support on the picket line (from trade unionists and from many feminists who identified with the women's movement rather than any particular trade union) but on 15 June local postal workers at Cricklewood started a boycott of Grunwick mail. Because Grunwick was a mail order photo processing plant it was totally dependent on postal services. At that stage victory for the strikers seemed a matter of weeks if not days.

It was this very situation – one where the workers themselves could take control of the struggle, organise and demand on their own behalf – which was not acceptable as far as the trade union bureaucracy and leadership were concerned. On the one hand the dispute was escalating through mass action into a head-on dispute with the government and employers; on the other hand, the trade union leadership with their job of negotiating (or compromising) between the workers and the bosses were becoming redundant. Their reaction was predictable. On 23 June, Roy Grantham, General Secretary of APEX, called for a limit of 500 on the number of pickets, and on 24 June, the TUC issued the following statement:

It would be a tragedy if the use of violence or any confusion introduced by irregular elements on the picket lines were to divide and deflect the support given by responsible trade unionists all over the country aimed at achieving an early and a peaceful solution to this problem. Trade unionists cannot condone the use of violence in this or any industrial dispute situation. At the same time, the TUC repeats its concern at allegations of unnecessary use of force by police against *bona fide* pickets.

As the Socialist Challenge pamphlet *The Battle of Grunwick*

commented, 'it was not made clear whether the TUC condoned
the use of "unnecessary force" against non *bona fide* pickets or
whether it thought the police were justified in using necessary
force. What was made clear was the TUC's opinion that the
control of the dispute must remain firmly in the hands of the
APEX executive. The statement went on to give full support to
APEX's decision to limit the number of pickets; the TUC wished
to stress to all trade unionists that any action by them should be at
the union's official request. No action should be taken without
contacting APEX Head Office at Wimbledon. (There was no
mention of contacting the strike committee at Brent).' The TUC
edict was followed on 5 July by action against the Cricklewood
sorters – they were laid off by the Post Office management and
threatened with the withdrawal öf strike pay by the Union of Post
Office Workers and as a result were forced to go back to handling
Grunwick mail. (Eventually these postal workers were to be fined
up to £500 for disobeying union orders, while on the same
occasion members who had disobeyed strike instructions elsewhere were fined much smaller sums).

The government responded to the unacceptable strength of the
mass picket by setting up a Court of Enquiry (under Lord Justice
Scarman) while at the same time condemning the 'violence' of the
pickets. Merlyn Rees visited the Grunwick police line on 27 June
and commented 'I learnt in Northern Ireland that operational
control must be left in the hands of the police.' The aim of the
mass picket had been to pressurise trade union leaders to cut off
essential supplies to the factory. It would have been an illegal
boycott, but was seen by the strikers as essential for victory.
However, the TUC was careful to keep well away from the whole
issue of such a boycott and the Court of Enquiry now provided
them with yet another excuse to defer any further action. When
the Scarman Enquiry finally reported on the 25 August, their
recommendations – in favour of union recognition and reinstate-
ment of the strikers – were, like the ACAS report, duly and legally
ignored by the Grunwick management. Like the ACAS report,
the Scarman report sank without a trace but it had already
fulfilled its function – that of sapping the strength and momentum
of the struggle. Six days later the TUC Congress finally called
weakly for 'practical aid' to the strikers but refused to commit
itself to cutting off supplies.

On the 22 November four members of the strike committee
(among them two women, Jayaben Desai and Yasu Patel) went

on hunger strike outside the headquarters of the Trade Union Congress in London. They were immediately suspended from APEX and had their strike pay taken away. To the strikers this last step on the part of the union bureaucracy was in line with the rest of their action. When asked, just after they ended their hunger strike, what impact it had had on the TUC Jayaben Desai replied (quoted from *Race and Class*, Winter 1977):

It had no impact. Oh they (the TUC) talk – they make rules and regulations; we can't make any hunger strike we can't make any demonstration, we can't make any mass picket, can't do anything. Now it means they are going to tie the workers' hands, and we shall have no chance to do anything. It means it will apply to everybody, not just to Grunwick strikers.
Q. How do you feel about your temporary suspension from APEX because of the hunger strike

It is a very bad thing. The union views itself like management. There's no democracy there, its strikers have no right to do anything. The union says that we have to accept everything that they say. We are the real fighters, the ones who came out of the company to fight for our rights. But the union just look on us as if we are employed by them. They have done the same thing to us as Ward did – they suspended us. And now we have to fight to be reinstated in the union and then also to be reinstated in the company.

The trade union leadership remained unmoved but to quote *Race and Class* (Winter 1977):

Where indeed can they move to? Their 'procedures' – ACAS, tribunals, industrial courts of enquiry – have been revealed as powerless and inadequate. To support the strikers effectively, which is their duty and responsibility, would entail breaking the law, or at least risk doing so. But this is ruled out on a number of counts. Such potential law breaking would threaten the deal between the Labour government and the unions – an agreement whose stability is crucial to government policy and the government's continued existence. For the trade unions to buck existing laws (eg. to cut off supplies to the factory) would involve them in a political struggle they do not have the strength or will to win – against the government, against the employers, against 'public opinion'. The only alternative, in the face of their own inability to act, is to get the government to fight for them – through demanding *laws* to back up current procedures. But this goes against all trade union traditions: invoking laws and the courts has been seen as an infringement of workers' freedom of action and power of collective bargaining. Also, whilst trade union leaders might want or need laws to strengthen procedures of 'conciliation', this might well rebound, since the management side of the dispute, supported by the misnamed National Association For Freedom (NAF), will also be pressing for laws – but to curtail workers' rights. NAF, Grunwick boss George Ward and the mass media have succeeded in shifting the emphasis of the dispute away from the right to join a union and the treatment of black workers to a debate on the tools of working-class struggle generally; the closed shop and the picket. . . . Black workers in this dispute have learned that because of their lack of numbers they alone cannot defeat their employers. They need the rank and file of the working class, which, through trade union structures and traditions has been acclimatised away from mass action. It is precisely because black workers have been kept away from these structures that they are now at the forefront of what has become one of the most political disputes in industrial history.

As this book goes to press, ACAS are said to be 'trying again'. The Grunwick dispute is still nominally dragging on. But such is the treacherous role of the trade union leadership that the victory over Grunwick management which had once seemed so near is now likely never to be realised. But the strikers who have fought over so many months with so much courage and strength have achieved another kind of victory – they have exposed once and for all the myth of the TUC's solidarity with exploited workers and in the process of doing so they have redefined the methods and outlook of industrial struggle.

The lesson of the Imperial Typewriters dispute had been (to quote the Asian workers strike committee statement):

Our struggle has taught us also that black workers must never for a moment entertain the thought of separate black unions. They must join the existing unions and fight through them. Where the unions fail in their duties to black workers they must be challenged to stand up for their rights. The union is an organisation of all workers, regardless of race, colour or sex. Right now the trade union movement in Britain is function-ing as a white man's union and this must be challenged. In challenging this we believe in the unity of the working class. This unity must be solidly established in deed and not only in words. It is the main task of the trade-union movement to create this unity.

At Grunwick this unity of the working class was achieved. Hundreds of trade unionists came day after day to support the Grunwick strikers on the picket line. But in the end it wasn't enough because they hadn't the courage to confront and defy the handful of men who control the trade union bureaucracy. The white working class had been weakened by their dependence on these leaders. They had grown unaccustomed to using their power of collective action. To remedy this weakness – that is the next task before the labour movement.

IV
Immigration

In Britain the most brutal, and wide ranging racism which occurs day after day is not the work of fascist minority parties but of Her Majesty's Government. It is the racism written into, and demanded by, Britain's immigration laws. New black immigration has long ago been stopped, but any black man or woman who wants to bring dependants over, or be visited by relatives from home, is now afraid of what these people will have to suffer.

English family relationships are said to be less strong than those of Asians, but most English people would be deeply shocked if their grandmother or grandfather, coming to visit them, or their young brother or sister, was held in detention by people with quasi-police powers, accused of lying and then sent back; or if their husband or wife, coming to join them after a long separation, was further delayed for years and then told that they were not the people they claimed to be and hence had no right to come at all. But that is just what is happening to black people coming to Britain as dependants and visitors. As for the women, the government seems not to regard them as human beings at all, unless as in the days of the British Empire the fact that they are women can be used to deny them basic rights or torture them in special ways.

Take the case of Shanaz Begum. In March 1977, at the age of sixteen, she had come from her village in a remote part of Pakistan to marry a cousin who had settled in Britain for many years. When she arrived at Heathrow airport, Immigration Officers interrogated her. They claimed that she was not yet sixteen and so could not marry and hence had no right to be here. She was taken to Harmondsworth detention centre and locked up. She had been there about a week when I learnt of her arrival through a friend and went to visit her. Her relations were keen that I should meet her, perhaps because they hoped in desperation that I might be able to help her. Unfortunately I could do nothing at all.

Harmondsworth detention centre is in an arid wasteland of motorways and outposts of the air terminals past Heathrow airport. It is a part of the grim complex called Government Buildings. To enter you must ring a bell, which sounds like a fire alarm and summons the Securicor men who guard the building and whom it is a criminal offence to 'obstruct in execution of the Immigration Act'. Opposite the front door a notice warns 'No food, alcohol or cameras.'

Inside is a long, uncarpeted prison-like corridor with bedrooms on either side of it, a television lounge which is furnished in the drabbest possible manner and a recreation room which contains nothing but a few wooden chairs and tables. There is also a yard where one could at one time sit and look at the adjacent buildings through the barbed wire. But the barbed wire has now been boarded up, presumably because the detainees must neither look out nor be seen from outside.

In this detention centre, contemptuous and inhuman attitudes have hardened into set rules. The bedrooms are kept locked from 9 am. to 9 pm. Often even young children can't have a comfortable nap during the day. If you are taken to Harmondsworth after a long journey and several hours of interrogation by Immigration Officers, there is nowhere for you to lie down and rest. And when you do finally get to bed, you can't lock yourself in and you may be woken up at any time of the night on any pretext.

Securicor guards and Immigration Officers can treat people as they wish. In 1975 a securicor guard at Harmondsworth told me (as I wrote in an article in the *Guardian*) 'Sometimes in this place people are naughty and we have to lock them in.' What does being naughty mean? I asked. 'Abusing us, being violent, trying to break out,' he told me.

But sobbing your heart out also counts as being naughty, which is what Demetroulla Karaiskou (a Cypriot girl) was locked up for. She had come to visit her sister for the third year running and, as 'on the three previous occasions, hoped to stay for a month. But her third visit came a little after the Cyprus coup, when British Immigration officers started suspecting all Cypriots of being potential immigrants.

Then again you may be taken from the detention centre to Pentonville Prison and locked up there if you complain. That is what happened to Owais Jeevanjee, a nineteen-year-old Asian with a British passport. He had complained about the way a mother and her child were being treated at Harmondsworth.

During 1975 and 1976 the detention centres would often get

crowded. Harmondsworth, which normally holds about forty men, women and children, would sometimes have up to four cots per small room. In 1977, work on an extension had begun. It was to provide, I was told, an extra wing for female detainees. Obviously the government intends to hold a larger number of women in detention in the future.

It was in this prison that I met Shanaz. She was sitting at a table in the recreation room with her relatives round her. She was startlingly beautiful, with proud elegant Kashmiri features and eyes so sensitive and expressive that the pain and humiliation she had suffered struck me, too, like a knife. She wore her bridal clothes and jewellery: this was how her mother had sent her, for the first time, from her home, taking care that every detail of her ornaments should be perfect – hoping, praying that she would be happy. But things went wrong right from the moment she landed in Britain. Although in law a female fiancée can enter Britain quite freely (without an entry certificate) she had been held up, questioned again and again, and late in the evening she had been given a sexual examination by officials who she thought might be doctors.

'There were two of them,' she said, 'both men, one of them was white, the other was probably a Pakistani. He spoke Urdu. He taunted me, asking me if I knew what was going to happen to me on my wedding night. Later they told me that the examination had shown that I was not yet sixteen and that I was to be sent back on the next flight.'

Shanaz's relations asked their MP to intervene, and while he made representations to the Minister with special responsibility for Immigration (Shirley Summerskill, Britain's representative at the United Nations Status of Women Conference) she was kept in detention. After a few weeks the final – and expected – decision was made and Shanaz was sent back to Pakistan, frightened and uncertain about the future.

Shanaz was not alone in suffering the humiliation of un-necessary sexual examination. Even during her time at Harmondsworth there were other women who had the same experiences. In fact it seemed that at that time (early 1977) sexual examination had become common practice at Heathrow Immigration Department, apparently carried out at the whim of the officials. I was told by Mary Dines, former General Secretary of the Joint Council for the Welfare of Immigrants, that, in the past, 'it was a fairly frequent occurrence that these young girls,

straight from their grandmothers' houses, would be taken to
Holloway prison, their pubic hair shaved off, and examined for
VD.' Most of these girls were not fiancées but daughters, come to
join their parents; the internal examinations were used to claim
that they were too old to come as dependants. There were cases
where parents disowned a daughter because the medical report
stated that she was not a virgin. But the frequency with which
women were thus brutalised depended not on the category of
entrant they fell into but on whether Immigration Officers wanted
to use these methods, and on the attitude of the Minister
responsible.

Under the Summerskill regime it seems that officials can
indulge in any sort of brutality they like. Summerskill's
predecessor, Alex Lyon, exercised a different kind of control.
Racism was not wiped out when Lyon was minister, on the
contrary some of the worst cases of human suffering at the hands
of Immigration Officers occurred in his regime, but he did
occasionally act with some humanity. He regarded himself as a
liberal and a 'friend of black people'. If representations were made
to him, by, for example, MPs, about specific cases, Lyon often
intervened to help the people involved. In his own words he was
'seeking to get immigration control on a basis where it was firm
but where it was administered with some degree of compassion
for the individual case'. But if you want to be humane you don't
last long as Minister with Special Responsibility for Immigration
because the policies you have to carry out are so inhumane. Lyon
was sacked soon after Callaghan became Prime Minister. The net
outcome of his days in office were that about two hundred of the
cases which were brought to his attention were treated with
regard for human dignity, but the law affecting the rights of
dependants and visitors was not changed (except for one fairly
minor aspect: in 1974 the sexually discriminatory 'Husbands
Rule' was changed to allow women born or settled in Britain to
have their foreign husbands here with them).

Even now people can be excluded or detained literally because
an Immigration Officer says he is 'not satisfied' about the person's
intentions. Even now for a Pakistani, Indian or Bangladeshi
woman waiting to join her husband in Britain it is not a matter of
getting a ticket and boarding a plane. She must wait months, if
not years, for an interview with an Entry Clearance Officer at a
British diplomatic mission on the Indian subcontinent, go
through endless interrogations about such subjects as the colour

of the family's goat or the number of rooms in the house she lives in or how many guests there were at the wedding and what happened on the wedding night. Other members of her family are also asked the same questions, and if there is the slightest discrepancy it can be used as proof that she is not the person she claims to be. The women I spoke to who had been through the whole procedure told me of the many exhausting visits they had had to make to the British Embassies and High Commissions, of the atmosphere of contempt at these places, of the pettiness of the Entry Clearance Officers (ECOs) and interpreters, and the rude and unreasonable questions they had had to answer. They told me that sexual examination is a routine part of the entry certificate procedure at British Diplomatic missions in the Indian subcontinent. When I asked Alex Lyon about this in an interview in early 1976 his answer was:

They do have a medical examination as part of the process of coming here and in the course of that medical examination it is sometimes disclosed that a woman is or is not a virgin, and that is sometimes noted on the medical report and from time to time some ECO's have used that piece of evidence in making a decision about the relationship of the wife; I have always condemned it and by and large it does not happen.
Q. Do you approve of a woman having to have a vaginal examination as a part of the routine medical examination to enter Britain?
A. The fact of the matter is that medical examination is carried out to see if they have any communicable disease. If they do, it is thought unwise to allow them to come and settle in this country by and large. If they had a communicable disease and it entailed investigating the vagina to find out, then I suppose the doctor is entitled to do that.

This firm statement of principle looks even more impressive when one considers that white women entering Britain are not subjected to these examinations.

But it is not enough to single out this or that Minister, or even the officials responsible. The reasons for the brutality and racism which are displayed every day at the ports of entry in Britain and at the British High Commissions in the Indian subcontinent are the laws themselves – laws which are seen as essential to wider government policy and which though blatantly racist (in fact they would not stand up before the Race Relations Act) were each introduced as a contribution to good community relations. In the last fifteen years successive laws have provided a continuing escalation in racism, irrespective of the government which brought them in. In fact Labour governments (in 1965 and 68) have been at pains to prove that they are just as good at keeping out the blacks as the Tories.

Right from the beginning the Immigration Laws have been an attack on black people as workers. They are designed not only to keep out black people but to try and intimidate black workers already in Britain and make it harder for them to claim their basic human rights. The 1971 Act finally put an end to black people settling in Britain by putting all incoming Commonwealth Citizens on a par with 'aliens'.

Aliens have long been the most vulnerable section of the British workforce. They are subject to a work permit system which ties them to one job and makes them dependent on their employers' goodwill to continue their stay in Britain. They are also denied the statutory right to bring their dependants or claim supplementary benefits. If they lose their jobs, instead of going on the dole they have to leave the country. The government had long preferred these white 'aliens' (with these low social costs) to Commonwealth immigrants (for example in 1969 the number of work permits issued to aliens was 67,788 compared to 3,512 vouchers for Commonwealth citizens). The 1971 Immigration Act means that if any new Commonwealth immigrants are admitted to Britain it will be on these exploitative and precarious terms.

The 1971 Act has also added new conditions which further weaken black workers – people can now be deported on grounds of 'general undesirability', and 'illegal immigrants' can be removed without a hearing. The Act has also vastly increased the powers of Immigration Officers. They can operate anywhere in the country and can arrest 'illegal immigrants' on suspicion and without a warrant. There have been several cases in the last few years in which police and Immigration Officers have raided factories and taken workers away. In refusing people admission at the airport, Immigration Officers have to obtain the approval of an Inspector in direct contact with the Home Office. But as an ex-Immigration Officer told the magazine *Race Today* (June 1973) 'If you don't show a good record in refusing people it is thought you are not doing your job properly.'

Having created a viciously oppressive system of laws and rules, the government has found the right sort of people to operate it. That Immigration Officers should be National Front members may seem utterly wrong to some people but not to the Home Office. When it was discovered that a member of the Immigration Department was in the National Front his seniors merely glossed over it, saying that he was not a permanent member and in any case it did not affect the way he carried out his duties.

But what is it like to face Immigration Officers when you come to Britain for the first time, not knowing the language, uncertain about the future? This is what happened to Zahira Galiara, a girl of eighteen from Bardoli, a village near Bombay.

In January 1976 she had an arranged marriage to a cousin Aszal who had settled in Britain and on October 20 that year the couple arrived in Britain. They arrived at 1 pm. and were held up by Immigration Officers. Aszal had all the documents required from a returning immigrant, but he was questioned for four hours and made to wait for four hours and then told he could go. But Zahira was told she had no right to enter, because although the couple had a marriage certificate she had no entry certificate. She was heavily pregnant but she was questioned and made to wait for the next twelve hours without food or water. Aszal refused to leave her until, he says, at 1 a.m. they were told that she had to go to a detention centre where men were not allowed. They were also told that at 10 o'clock next morning she would be put on a plane back to India.

Zahira was taken by car to Harmondsworth detention centre. 'I was taken to a room which I had to share with three others, two Indian women and one black man,' she told me. 'I just lay there, completely exhausted. I could not sleep and the pains started.' In the morning Zahira had quite severe labour pains. She was taken to Queens' Building detention centre at the airport where Aszal was waiting for her. They asked to see a doctor and Zahira was taken to another part of the building where, she says, she was superficially examined by a doctor and a nurse. Although she speaks no English, Aszal was not allowed to accompany her. The doctor's opinion was that she was fit to travel. The Galiaras were told that she would be put on a plane at 3.30 pm.

'When she came back from the doctor, she was crying in pain,' says Aszal Galiara. 'But the immigration officials and security men just laughed and said she was pretending because she didn't want to be sent back.'

Zahira's pains increased and she was screaming uncontrollably. Aszal says that he tried to call a doctor or an ambulance from the public telephone but was prevented from doing so by the guards. Only when the baby's head began to emerge from the womb was a doctor sent for.

'By the time he arrived,' says Aszal, 'the baby was half out, the only people to help were an Indian cleaning woman and myself.' Zahira and her baby were finally taken to Ashford hospital. But the baby, a girl, was premature and, according to the hospital, born with abnormalities.' She died soon after. Zahira was eventually given permission to stay on in Britain.

Was it all really necessary? It could hardly have been the result of an error. Immigration Officers could see that Zahira was pregnant and, whether or not they thought the baby's birth imminent, they could hear her screaming in pain. Also, according to Aszal, they said they did not doubt that she was his wife. The Galiaras were told that all the trouble was caused by the fact that she had no entry certificate, but that does not explain the inhuman treatment she received.

The waiting period for Entry Certificates at the British Consulate in Bombay is more than a year. But why are entry certificates so essential for Asian wives and children who have a right to enter Britain? White immigrants from the Irish republic, EEC countries and even from Rhodesia come in with no such bureaucratic barriers.

In response to the article on Zahira's experiences which I wrote in the *Guardian* I got, in addition to the usual sick and abusive letters from racists, a number of letters from English women who sympathised with Zahira. Most of them enclosed letters to be forwarded to her. Their sentiments were all very similar, and this letter from Lincolnshire expresses them quite clearly:

I can hardly believe that anyone should behave so cruelly and insensitively to any woman expecting a baby, especially to one like you, almost alone in a strange land. Of course you will grieve for the loss of your child, but I hope you will soon find out how caring and considerate people usually are of a woman in these circumstances. Please do not judge us all by these ignorant officials.

A kind thought, but one which suggests that the 'fault' lies with the 'ignorant' official and no one else, that the whole affair was an exceptional accident rather than one product of a carefully constructed machinery which demands these attitudes in its operators. And in addition, since the writer disassociates herself and most 'caring and considerate people' from the people who caused Zahira's experiences, it suggests that nothing need be done to change the set-up which resulted in her tragic experience, that citizens whose government is racist and oppressive are in no way responsible for its policies.

What I have described so far applies to people direct from the Indian sub-continent. Those from East Africa are mainly British Citizens. They faced the 1968 Immigration Act. The purpose of this Act was to deny them their right, as British citizens, to enter Britain. It was the first official declaration that British passports mean nothing if their owners are black. Of course this was all achieved without using the words black and white. The Act divided holders of British passport into two categories – those who had 'substantial connection' with the UK, who could enter Britain without restriction, who were almost all white, and those who could not. Having been denied their statutory right as British citizens to enter Britain, those East African Asians who were actually being kicked out of East Africa were offered the chance to queue for quota vouchers for entry to Britain. A limited number of these vouchers were issued each year. What it meant in human terms was that black UK citizens excluded from their own country (Britain) were and still are being forced to live in countries where they have no right to live or work. Many have become ill and destitute, and those who have tried to enter Britain without a voucher have found themselves being shuttlecocked in and out of Britain or kept in prison. As Ian Macdonald points out in *The New Immigration Law* (Butterworths, 1972):

The International Commission of Jurists criticised the 1968 Act at the time of its passing as being in violation of international law. The existence of the Act would be a clear violation of the third protocol (not ratified by the UK) to the European Convention on human rights, which provides in article 3 that no one shall be deprived of the right to enter the territory of which he is a national. This undoubtedly prevents Britain ratifying the protocol; in addition the operation of the Act would appear to infringe certain articles of the existing European Convention . . . Yet despite all of this, the Immigration Act 1971 continues, albeit in a different form, the system of control instituted by the 1968 Act.

In fact, in regard to whom it allowed free entry into Britain, the 1971 Act differed mainly in the words used. Again, it avoided the words black and white but it classified people as patrials and non-patrials; in general terms, patrials, who can come and go as they wish, are almost always white; non-patrials are almost never white. Now the Green Paper on Nationality, effectively a first draft of the law on nationality which is to be introduced in 1978, confirms that the same concepts are to be retained. In the future, we are told, citizenship of the UK and colonies is to be abolished. It will be replaced by two new categories – British Citizenship and British Overseas Citizenship. 'The dividing line,' writes Ann Dummett in *British Nationality Law, a Briefing paper on the Government's Green Paper*, 'between the two is to be almost exactly the same as the line which under the 1971 Immigration Act separates UK and colonies citizens with a right of entry to the UK (patrials) from those citizens who are subject to immigration control (non-patrials).' In future, British citizens will have the right to enter the UK; British overseas citizens will not.

Among the groups of people who would become British Overseas citizens as soon as the law comes into force would be citizens of the UK and colonies who are living in present and former colonies and do not have British-born ancestors. This would include East African Asians who have been kept out of Britain all these years, and possibly the more recently arrived East African Asians in Britain. The residence period for a British Overseas Citizen to qualify as a British Citizen has not yet been specified, nor have the rights, if any, of British citizens already living in Britain. These people will have no right to enter Britain and no right either to work or vote in Britain or elsewhere. Their children will in many cases be born stateless (unless they happen to be born in a country where birth confers the right of citizenship). At present British single mothers cannot pass on their citizenship to children born abroad, nor can married women pass on their citizenship to children born abroad with non-UK fathers. Both these points will be remedied if the proposals of the Green Paper are accepted. But married women who are British Overseas citizens will have very few such rights. This is in line with immigration laws which have been blatantly sexually discriminatory against black women. For example, the 1971 Act prevents single mothers from bringing their children into Britain unless they can prove sole responsibility; and a woman can never be regarded a 'head of a household' unless her husband is mentally or physically handicapped.

These laws, with their impersonal jargon, may seem disconnected from reality, but in fact they are a far more destructive attack on black people than any activities of the National Front. They have destroyed hundreds of lives – of the women separated for ever from their husbands, of young children forcibly kept from their mothers and old parents left in isolation because they don't qualify as dependants. It is these laws which have been used to humiliate tired and defenceless visitors, to deport workers without even a hearing, to lock innocent people in prison and brand them criminals, and to provide employers with a work-force made powerless through legislation.

As for the position of Asian women, the immigration laws show the government's attitude – that there is no need even to pretend that they are equal. The implication in all the sexually discriminatory immigration laws (continued long after the intro- duction of the Sex Discrimination Act in 1975) is that women are slaves and chattels in their communities, and the government sees no reason why it should treat them as anything else. Married women's passports have hardly any value. Even if they are British citizens, they simply do not qualify to settle in Britain if their husbands are non-UK passport holders. They are expected to go and live in their husbands' countries. Their parents, brothers, and sisters may all be in Britain but they are still being excluded. If at all, they are allowed in only as temporary visitors. They could never bring their husbands, because to do so, they would have to be considered as a head of a household, something which, as I have said earlier, no woman can be unless her husband is dead, or mentally or physically incapacitated. As for their children, they would not be allowed to live in Britain for any length of time, and while they were here they would be prevented from attending school.

This is how one woman, Feroza, described her experience. Her sister was present during the interview.

Originally I was from Uganda. I don't know if it was my hard luck or what, but I married a Pakistani. I had gone for further studies to Pakistan and I got married there. When I got married I was only seventeen and my husband was twenty-one. I wanted to marry him. My parents explained to me, Pakistan is too far from this country (Uganda), you are not used to their ways, but I didn't listen to them. We are Muslims and my husband is my cousin, so from the point of view of tradition it is all right for me to marry him.

After my marriage I used to go to Africa every one and a half years or so. My parents, brothers and sisters were all in Africa. The last time I went there was in 1968; after that I couldn't go there because I was a British citizen. My family moved to Britain, and because of the distance and the expense I could not visit them. For seven years I didn't see them. There was such loneliness. I had nobody of my own in Pakistan. We lived in Rakant near Rawalpindi. Before my marriage I used to be very active and very talkative but after my marriage, when I went to Pakistan – there you have to wear the *Burkha*. I had never worn that thing before. After my marriage I realised that I would have to use it, put it on whenever I went out. We lived with my in-laws, and in their house even girls as young as my daughter (12) have to use it.

Her sister said: 'She was born in Uganda, brought up and educated there. It is difficult to change yourself.'

Feroza continued:

I didn't say anything to my in-laws or my husband. I thought I'd absorb myself in all these things. But it didn't work. I started losing weight. When I left Uganda, my weight was 135 pounds, but in one year only 100 pounds were left, only bones were there.

Now after seven years separation I have come to see my family. And when I saw all of them after such a long time I didn't like to go back again, really I didn't want to at all. But the problem is that the government won't allow my children to go to school. I have brought them with me but I can't just keep them at home. They went to school in Pakistan. I don't know what to do with them. I am a British citizen but the Home Office don't want me to stay on here in spite of that.

The day I left Uganda my troubles started. I was only sixteen then. From that day to now, thirteen years, I haven't had any peace. All that peace I left in Uganda . . . When I left Uganda after my marriage, my mum told me, never write anything to me about your troubles because you didn't listen to us. It is all up to you – and I decided that I was never going to say anything to her because I had done it all on my own. And my elder brother, he had told me the same thing – 'Babi, you are not listening to us so we are not responsible for anything.' I was seventeen then so I said 'That's fine. I don't care'. I was very talkative before marriage but after marriage I don't know what happened to me. I became so quiet and lonely and sometimes I didn't even want to see my husband (after my daughter was born and when she was a baby).

My in-laws never asked me how I was. I tried to accept their ways and that affected me.

Her sister said:

The thing is her marriage was against her in-laws' wishes and against my parents'. She couldn't turn either way for help because she knew the answer would be 'it is your own fault'. So she left it all to herself and tried to carry on but it was too much for her. Now she has come to us. If she can stay, if her husband is allowed to join her, she can start a new life, with people who love her . . . Her in-laws don't accept her. The grudge is there and always will be. There is no point staying on there then, is there? If the husband is nice that's good but that's not enough, not all the time. You need other people.

Feroza (wiping her eyes) said: 'These tears come out all the time.' Her sister continued:

In Pakistan the boys are so very obedient to their families. All right, they say, a wife is a wife after all, but when it comes to a parents' decision . . . If the parents say your wife should do this or should not do that, the boy listens to his parents. For a couple to live apart from the in-laws in a village in Pakistan would be almost impossible.

Feroza continued:

There was almost no time of day when we could be together alone. It took me a few months to realise that my life was changed completely. In Uganda I used to wear very beautiful clothes but after my daughter's birth I don't know what happened to me. Do you understand what I am trying to tell you, that I was filled with distaste for everything? I didn't like anything, I felt like going away somewhere where no one would see me, not even my husband, I wanted to escape from my life itself. When I had lived in Uganda I was the first daughter, after five boys, my parents and brothers, they really loved me, they hardly refused me anything. But after marriage it was so different. I used to wonder why nothing I did was right. You know the *Burkha*, at first I couldn't wear it, I had never worn it before. Two or three times I fell down when I was wearing it, that was outside in the market place. I fell down. A grown woman falling down! I was overcome with shame. I thought, what has happened to me! What have I done with my life! Then I stopped going out. It was better not to go out than to go and fall down.

At home the attitude of my parents-in-law was that I was from outside Pakistan, so I must be very independent – although I never showed my independence. I was seventeen then and I loved my husband with so much intensity. It is not a good age to assess people or things. But my husband always thought that my in-laws were good to me, because they never criticised me in his presence. He had told them beforehand 'I know this girl, what she is like, so I don't want to hear anything about her from you. You mustn't ever try to talk to me about her or I'll leave the home.' Many wives complain to their husbands about petty things which happen during the day, but I never did. Even when I felt really bad I would keep quiet, and this affected my body. I became very weak, I could not sleep or feel any hunger or desire to speak to anyone.

In Uganda I had always been keen on the latest styles, trying new clothes from week to week. I had so many clothes but my mother never said no to more. I was always keen on dressing up and going out to meet my friends. In Pakistan all that changed, all I wanted was the bed on which to lie alone. I used to wear a bra the same size as my mother's, size 40 it used to be, but I just seemed to dry up completely. My clothes hung on me as though they had been draped on a piece of wood. Gradually I lost the courage to speak out about anything or to question anyone; I started suffering from palpitations. My heart would suddenly start beating very fast as though my life was beating out of me. It lasted only 3 or 4 seconds. It started happening about once a fortnight, then about once a week. In the end I got to the state when it might happen three or four times a day. Since I came to England it has got much less.

My husband's family, although they are educated, – one of my brothers-in-law is a barrister and another is an engineer – they are still very narrow-minded about women. They didn't want me to wear saris. It is not that I wore sleeveless blouses – they were always long sleeved and not *Choli's* either but even then they disliked it. So I just folded my saris and put them away. When I left Uganda, people used to wear tight pyamas and Kamiz, but these too they did not approve of. So I gave them up, gave them all up. But in my mind I suffered. I couldn't help remembering the pleasure I had had in my clothes, how keen my mother had been on my wearing them, how we had often designed them and chosen them together and my mother had made most of them.

To go back to Pakistan again – it would be like dying. And when I think of my daughters growing up in that atmosphere, in that society, I feel I must try to avoid it if in any way I can. But I cannot live without my husband. I love him so much I cannot ever imagine leaving him. He was the first man I ever really looked at. Now every minute of the day I miss him. I am stricken with memories of him. He is prepared to come to Britain and live with me here but I do not know if he will be allowed. I am prepared to wait if I know that in the end he'll be let in, but in the meantime I just want them to allow my children to attend school. When I see other children going to school I feel so depressed and disturbed, my girl is indoors all day. When I took her to a school for admission they sent us to the Education department. I have been there three times, but each time they say I must go back to the Home Office and try to get my daughter a visa for longer than a six months' stay in Britain; otherwise she cannot be admitted to school. We have been in Britain more than a year now, so the Home Office has extended her visa, but each time they extend it it is only by three months or six months so that she is never eligible for school. All this trouble they are giving us despite the fact that I have a UK passport. If I am forced because of this to return – what then? But I don't even want to think about that, because if I do I begin to hate everything. I am afraid that one day I'll come to hate even my brothers and sisters. My hands become cold, my body becomes cold.

Some months after I spoke to Feroza I learnt that she had had to return to Pakistan. She had received the news that her husband was seriously ill and she and her children had rushed back to be with him. It is unlikely that she will be allowed into Britain again, even as a visitor.

V
School Life
'Don't you understand English or are you just stupid'

I asked a girl of twelve what she thought was the most important thing to stress in my book? She answered – 'The way people are treated! The way everyone is treated in this country.'

Schooldays are said to be the happiest days in your life but for Asian children in Britain they are often the harshest. Their pre-school life is often more sheltered than it is for white children. They may be deprived of skills and they may receive less stimulation than, say, middle-class English children, but inside the Asian family they get plenty of security and love. At five they are then pushed into an environment where the language is new, the rules incomprehensible and where, unless it is a predominantly Asian area, they are made to realise that they belong to a special category – Asian. And being an Asian is almost always made out to be a disadvantage.

The structure of primary education in Britain is implicitly racist – in the books used, the curriculum, the teachers' attitudes. But discussion of racism is taboo. When I asked the headmistress of a junior school my daughter had been attending about the racist remarks children at the school had been making her answer was well-meaning and typical: 'Asking them to say thank you and please or asking them not to swear is one thing but asking them not to say "nigger" or "wog" or "black people stink" is quite another. A discussion of these things would only make the atmosphere worse.' There *are* teachers who try to take a strong anti-racist line but they are exceptions, often fighting a lone and unsuccessful battle against the racism of the school system. Meanwhile, the majority of their colleagues prefer not to talk either about their own attitudes to race or about racism in their schools. Since in general 'politics' should not be discussed in school, it is easy for teachers to claim that they have no strong opinions about subjects like, say, the National Front. Often their private 'non-political' opinion is that the National Front are to be condemned as extremists; but since what the National Front is extreme about is racism, this implies that it is all right to be moderately racist. A reluctance to take a stand about racism, in fact indifference to it, has been shown again and again by head teachers. In December 1977 the Headmistress of St Anselm's School in Canterbury, one of Britain's leading Roman Catholic Comprehensives, allowed a teacher who was a National Front candidate to continue in her post after she had promised that her National Front views would not affect her treatment to black pupils.

As for the National Union of Teachers, they rejected a motion at their annual conference calling for the exclusion of National Front members from school teaching. Perhaps if the National Front had been excluded, the racism they stand for would have had to be faced up to, 'making it worse' for those very genteel people in charge of education.

But for Asian children, racism is impossible to ignore. School, with its white figures of authority, its totally foreign values and judgements, comes as a shock. After the initial effects of this wear off, children begin to realise their own and their parents' position. The rules of the education system, such as bussing and the reception class system (see later in this chapter), are only implicitly racist, but the way Asian children are actually treated in school is often quite overtly so. When a child gets out of line in assembly and the teacher shouts 'Don't you understand English or are you just stupid', or when Indian parents who do come to speak to teachers are laughed at or rebuffed, children both black and white learn just how Indians are thought of by people who matter. What these children face is a kind of colonial experience which they are far too young to fight against. The children under eleven I spoke to almost invariably had a sense of inferiority similar to that of a colonised people. They were ashamed of anything Indian. They disowned their food and their language and in some cases even their Indian first names. A few tried to make even their skin as inconspicuous as possible –as white as possible.

Interview with girl of nine from Southall:
Q. Would you like to go to India?
A. No, I wouldn't.
Q. Why not?
A. I don't think it is nice in India because sometimes when you come from India you get black.
Q. You don't want to get black?
A. No.

Q. Why not?

A. (touching her face) Because if someone's black, if you touch them in the face you might think your face might get black. It may be catching.

(Although the caste system in India has led to the attitude that it is more attractive to be light skinned than dark, this extreme fear of getting black does not exist in India or Pakistan.)

A teacher, again in a Southall primary school, told of an 'amusing' incident when an Indian girl of ten was reduced to tears when she had to go out in the sun in the summer term. She was afraid of becoming black.

This apparent rejection of one's race is often accompanied by a desire not to stand out, not to cause trouble, to tip-toe about hoping nobody will notice you. Why? Because this is not your country, because the British have done you a favour by letting you in.

It is an attitude which is known among adults too. A Sikh Conservative Councillor – Mr Mangat – expressed it quite clearly in 1973: 'The best hope for Sikhs in this country lies in abandoning the turban and making themselves as inconspicuous as possible. It would damage community relations and hinder the process of acceptance and integration if Sikhs looked conspicuous in the street.' (quoted by Geeta Amin in her B.Tech.Hons thesis *Asian Women in Southall, Political and Social Situation*). In Southall now, particularly since the murder in summer 1976 of a young man, Gurdeep Singh Chaggar, by racist thugs, few Asian adults even think about integration, let alone want it. But young children continue to absorb these racist opinions and their corrupting values.

Interview with Indian girl of nine who was born here and has never been to India:

Q. Do you think there are too many Indians in Southall?

A. Yes.

Q. Why?

A. Because every time I walk somewhere I see lots of Indians.

Q. Would you prefer to see English people?

A. Yes.

Q. Why

A. Sometimes I think where I walk is India.

Interview with Indian girl, eight years old:

Q. Are there too many Indians in Southall?

A. Yes.
Q. Why?
A. Suppose there is some shop, right. An English man owns it, an Indian man comes and buys it, right. With too many Indians all the Indians are getting spoilt, they start to do stealing and all.

Classically racist opinions – from Indian children!
For an Asian child growing up in Britain there is a choice. Either you stand outside your community, see them as non-Indians see them, which means, often enough, identifying with racist opinion, or you learn to hate people who say these things. Many children are caught in between. They lead a double life, on the surface passive, even servile, but inside they suffer.
In spring 1974 I was able to interview about 30 Asian, West Indian and English children between the ages of 8 and 11. They were on an outing from school – a day of activities organised by Scope Southall, an independent community organisation. I interviewed them individually and in a separate room. They were happy, relaxed children and seemed keen to talk to me about themselves. But when certain subjects were mentioned the Asian kids became silent, hesitant. One of these subjects was food.

Q. What is your favourite food?
A. (long pause) Don't know how to say it in English.
Q. Tell me in Gujerati.
A. (in almost a whisper) *Vatatebeda*.
[*With a little encouragement they tended to become more confident:*]
Q. What is your favourite food?
A. (uncertainly) I like chapatti and lentils.
Q. *Dal*, you mean.
A. Yes! And I like *Gobi ki Sabji* and chips and fish, that's all.

The day's activities included a slide show of photographs taken in and around Southall. When pictures of Indian sweet shops were shown, the English and West Indian children present sneered and made vomiting noises while the Asians watched in silent embarrassment.
That Asian children are teased about their food may not seem very important in itself, but it does rather lead to the thought – if people eat food which is thought of as disgusting and unclean what are these people like? And it provides a cover for racist fantasies such as these comments of primary school teachers –

'Southall stinks of curry' or 'I am always sneezing when I come here. It must be the curry.'

Children understand the true meaning of these remarks. An Indian girl of ten said: 'Some people think we've made Southall look horrible. We've made all our horrible Indian food and that.'

Only a minority of teachers I spoke to were interested in the way of life of their Asian pupils and an even smaller number knew anything about it. This lack of interest goes right through the educational system. In Ealing for example (an area where a high proportion of the population is Asian) not one school had facilities for teaching Asian languages. Of course an Asian child here must learn English, but must she or he forget their own language in order to learn English? A girl of ten told me that children in her school were punished if they spoke in their own language. An Indian teacher said that in his school Asian children's names were almost invariably mispronounced. But when in one class he had taken the register and pronounced their names correctly, there had been some laughter from non-Indian children (who were a minority in the class) but floods of embarrassed giggles from Asian children, who seemed to prefer their names to be mispronounced in school.

Indian language and Indian food are seen by whites as inferior, but religion is slightly different. It is seen not as a racial characteristic but as identical with race. Jesus is seen as British and belonging to the British. One English girl of nine asked me 'Coloured people believe in our God, but do you Indians believe in him or do you have a God of your own?' Religious instruction in most schools is not really conducive to respect for non-Christian religions. Children in primary school are often told stories from the Old Testament. Whether these are presented as interesting old stories or as moralistic and relevant fables depends on the attitude of the head teacher. Teachers often choose to stress that the 'baddies' in these stories are 'idol-worshippers'. And everyone knows that such 'idol-worshippers' abound in the 'East'.

I spoke to Sikh and Hindu children in Southall and none of them had been withdrawn from religious education lessons. Some children from Hindu families even attended Sunday school, mainly because there was nothing much else to do at weekends. An Indian girl of ten said:

I used to go to Sunday school but I don't go any more. If you went to Sunday school every week you could go to the seaside free. But if you miss only two or three weeks then you pay a little money — 23p, I think it is. I used to go to Sunday school all the time before and they said I could go free. Then I began to go to the temple and I didn't go to Sunday school any more, because I had been to the seaside lots and lots of times — the same one every time.

'English' prayers were seen by these Asian children (mainly Sikhs and Hindus) as innocuous, even in some cases enjoyable, but not of any emotional significance. They often seemed to feel that 'Indian' prayers didn't belong in the world of school. Only one child, a Sikh girl of ten, had attempted to say non-Christian prayers in school.

Q. Are you religious? Do you say prayers?
A. Yes, in assembly while they say it in English I do the other one. We have to say the English one and I hate saying da-da-da so I make my own one, an Indian prayer and say it.
Q. What do the others say about that?
A. They don't like it. One day we had a fight and they told Miss. Miss said it was all right for me to say my own prayer. Me and Karin, my friend, we do that.

Muslim children in general have a slightly different attitude to religious education in school. This is because of two main differences between Islam and Hinduism or Sikhism. Firstly Muslims (like Christians and unlike Hindus) have set prayers which should be said during the day, so that Christian prayers can be regarded as a threat or at least an alternative to Islam, and secondly, while Hindu and Sikh parents often regard Christian prayers for their children as so much water off a duck's back, Muslims, again like Christians or religious Jews, object to any other religious influence on their children. Because of this, when Muslim children are not withdrawn from religious education lessons it is usually because the parents are not aware of these lessons. 'Religious identification,' writes Afshan Begum in her thesis *Adolescent Muslim girls in British Schools*, 'is generally much stronger among Muslims.' But according to a report *Education and Single Sex Schools* (compiled by the union of Muslim organisations in the UK), quoted by Afshan Begum;

. . . an extremely small number of Muslim children have been withdrawn from religious education and morning worship in the past. Although the

Act (sec. 25, 1944 Education Act) would seem to give parents and pupils the right to practise a religion other than that [Christianity], in general there is little or no provision made in school for any kind of peripatetic Muslim teacher to give lessons in Islam.

Children between eight and twelve seem too young to fight against cultural racism in school; it is as though they are almost stunned into accepting the inferiority with which white society has labelled them. But at twelve their feelings seem to change. It is not that racism vanishes — in fact it intensifies and violence increases, but most children start to face up to it at this point, and their 'inferiority' usually clears away. After all, when racism takes the form of violence, they can't fail to recognise it as an attack on themselves, and part of a value system they cannot go along with. Also, with puberty, children, especially girls, begin to develop their own sense of identity. Previously their view of Britain was conditioned by their parents' expectations. Now they can reject these and look back more objectively at the implicitly racist atmosphere of their primary school days.

In Southall bussing and reception classes go on through secondary school. Geeta Amin and I have described some of the effects of reception class in secondary schools as they were in 1974 (*Guardian* 15 Aug. 1974):

When immigrant children first enter the borough they are sent, if the education department has any doubts about their English, to an assessment centre, and from there a large proportion of them are channelled into reception classes. They stay in the reception classes for a period of up to three years, after which they are usually dropped into the lowest streams of the schools to which the classes are attached . . . East African Asian children are sent for assessment even when they speak fluent English . . . The fact that reception classes are lumped with the remedial department sharpens the image which English children have of them. The class, located as it usually is in a prefabricated hut at the bottom of the school garden, is seen as inferior. We were told by English boys that reception classes were 'like Junior schools with pictures on the walls' and that the work done in them was not really serious. The boys could see that in reception classes, as in the all-in village school of a few generations ago, only one teacher taught all subjects to children between twelve and sixteen. This was taken as proof that the class was inferior to, and separate from, the main school.

According to teachers, the school was divided into three social groups, which didn't mix: English children, Indian children in the main school, and reception class children. In the frequent racial fights, reception class children are usually the targets. When reception class children fight back, schools take drastic measures to avoid clashes. In two Northolt schools, for example, Indian children were sent home half an hour early every day last term. This meant they missed virtually a whole period every day. Reception class children involved in fights have also been moved to schools outside the area 'for their own safety', we were told by teachers. The children's version was 'they were chucked out because they fought back.'

The position of Asian children in secondary schools in and around Southall is made worse by bussing. They are literally outsiders in the schools they attend, miles away from their homes. Their gathering for the bus ride home is often the occasion for a racial attack. In October 1975 a Pakistani boy of fifteen was killed by a gang of white boys at a bus stop.

The anger among Asian teenagers which Geeta and I noticed in 1974 has of course since then led to Asian boys hitting back. For them the role of victim of white gangs is over. But now there is a new kind of racial violence in schools – girls attacking girls. Girls of twelve to fifteen I spoke to in Harlesden said that the worst aspect of their lives was the bullying and racism they faced in school. Sharmi (twelve) said:

They call you Paki, things like that, and if you answer back then you are really in serious trouble. Then they get their friends on you, they beat you up. If you report it, that's worse still! None of the Indian girls complain, because they are afraid of being beaten up, so none of them go up to the headmaster and complain.

In schools in this area, the girls told me there were three social groups, West Indian, English and Irish, and Asian. 'There is hostility between West Indians and English,' they told me, 'they don't mix much, they keep apart, though sometimes there are fights. But attacks on Asian girls are much more common.'

Quite apart from the violence, the girls told me it was difficult to be friendly with white girls. Sharda (fifteen) said:

They usually talk about their boyfriends; we haven't got any to talk about. If they talk about their homes, their homes are completely different from ours. We accept what they say, but if we talk about our homes — my mum said this or I cooked this — they hardly understand what we are saying. We have to explain every single thing. They want to know how or what for, about every thing, then at the end they say 'Rubbish!' and they tease and tell other people. We eat with our fingers – they think that is dirty and disgusting.

Relations with West Indian girls seemed no better. Tara, a fourteen-year-old, told me of a sequence of events which, her friends agreed, was hardly an exception:

A girl in my class, just because one coloured girl doesn't like her everybody gangs up against her. They used to really flatten her down. Now they don't talk to her. Nobody talks to her. Before, every time there was games they would kick her and everything. When she complained, she'd had it. She had to stay off school for two or three weeks.

However Sharda had a close friend who was West Indian and she had discussed with her the reasons why Asian girls were so frequently attacked and bullied:

I have a Jamaican friend, she says there should be no difference if someone is West Indian, Indian or African, we are all black. She says that we Indians are not 'strict' enough. She says 'If a coloured girl tells you off, you are a grown-up, you should give it back.' I say 'I might be the only one, while she has five friends.' That's the trouble, Indians are just one on their own. But coloured girls, they make a gang and defend each other or beat others up . . . If only we could be like that! Then things would change. West Indians never went to self-defence classes but they can still beat us up. It is co-operation with each other that is most important. It is also very difficult to get. Sometimes I myself am not sure if I could do it. If I saw an Indian girl being beaten up, I might just watch or walk away. My Jamaican friend, if she saw a coloured girl being beaten, she would run to help her. Even if she doesn't know her, hasn't seen her before.

East African Asians told me that West Indians sometimes behave as though they are superior to Asians, because Asians are religious or because Asians can't speak English well. However, an Asian community worker in North London told me 'West Indian children arc only reacting to the insufferable cultural superiority that Asians feel. Indian culture is a big barrier and they make it more so by always thinking they are superior.' Both these opinions were repeated to me by many people and both seemed likely to be true. In addition, as one white secondary school teacher told me 'It is a matter of style. In the eyes of children, West Indians have it and Asians don't. When a West Indian boy walks in, the girls look up; they don't do that for an Asian. In our school there is no doubt there is a hierarchy. The West Indians are at the top and the Asians are at the bottom.'

But a more powerful reason for conflict than all these is the British education system itself, with its essentially ethnocentric curriculum, its apathy, its built-in attitude that Western culture is the only culture and its pervasive mockery of people who are 'different'. It is a system insidious but extremely powerful, where pupils may end up learning quite a lot about the way of life in ancient Rome and Greece but nothing about the way of life of their fellow pupils who are black. It is a system where a reasonably educated person would have heard of Homer but never of Kalidas, of Ibsen but rarely of Tagore, of Joan of Arc but not of the Rani of Jhansi (another woman who took arms to try to drive the British out of her country), of Goethe but not of his contemporary the great Urdu poet Mirza Ghalib. This ignoring of non-European high culture and history may not seem important, but it is a part of the same ethos which permits the everyday culture of Asian life to be stamped on so viciously in schools. This is what a small thing, cooking a few Indian dishes in a Willesden school, led to. Sharmi told me the story:

Mrs X—— (a teacher) used to like Indian food and there were quite a few Indian girls in the class, so in two or three lessons in the cookery class they made Indian food. They made chapattis and everything. They brought some things from home as well. Mrs. X said 'I don't mind if you use my pots and pans'. Then after two lessons some second year girls came over. They said 'It stinks, it's disgusting, it's horrible stuff!' . . . When they say directly to you it stinks or something like that, you get hurt inside of you. People start crying. They really start crying. It is not a pretty sight to see people so hurt. So after it happened a few times our teacher said 'We won't have cooking like this any more.' She stopped cooking. She said 'there'll be no cooking except the things I have to teach – things like cakes.'

The girls I spoke to rarely discussed their problems at school with their parents. Their mothers, they told me, often complained when they didn't want to take any food to school for their lunch. But even that had not been discussed in detail at home. The reason was that as a result of bullying some Asian children were afraid to eat Indian food at school. It is only in cases of the most violent attacks that parents get to know what has been happening, because, as the girls told me 'we don't like to worry them about it.

They have enough problems without this.' Or 'in our house we don't like to talk about racism, everyone is tired in the evenings and we don't like to talk about it.' Or 'my parents are not educated, they won't understand.'

At the back of their minds many girls feel that perhaps, even if they told their parents, they would fail to understand, or take in a situation so different from their own educational experiences. Girls from orthodox Muslim and Sikh families feel this most strongly; they also fear that through some misunderstanding their parents might try to withdraw them from school altogether, cutting off their lifeline to the outside world. Some of these girls whose families have come from rural areas in Azad Kashmir or Mirpur feel that their parents allow them to go to school only because in Britain it would be illegal for them to remain at home. To criticise the school system in these circumstances would be not only pointless but risky.

Asian parents' attitudes to their daughter's education vary tremendously with their religion, background in Pakistan or India, and, of course, with the people involved. The progressives, like their contemporaries in towns and cities in India, frequently have hopes and dreams for their daughters' academic success. Often they plan out careers for these girls without even consulting them. This is how Meena, a Gujerati Hindu girl whose family come from Bombay, described her parents' attitudes:

My parents, and most Asian parents, they live for their children. Everything they do is for their children. They have so many hopes and dreams for their children's future. When it doesn't come out the way they want it to, that is when they get most hurt I think . . . They wanted me to be a secretary and they wanted my sister to be a doctor or something medical. I don't know why they decided it that way. When we went to visit relations my dad would say 'She is going to be a doctor and she is going to be a secretary.' It turned out to be nearly the opposite (laughs). My sister is a secretary and I am studying biology. It's funny really, now he doesn't say a word.

Parents confirmed these attitudes. A woman from Nairobi who is a laundry worker in North London but whose husband works in a bank told me about her daughter. 'She is really intelligent and she is going to make something of her life, I know. She is very good at her studies and we want her to be a teacher. I think she'll succeed.' In contrast to this, among Muslim families, particularly those from a peasant background, the daughter's education is considered irrelevant. In extreme cases, say of a family from the remote rural areas of Azad Kashmir, if the mother has just had a baby, it is known for daughters of twelve to stay at home from school for weeks, do all the cooking, look after the younger children and generally run the home. Between these two poles of urban progressive Gujerati families and Muslim peasant families fall the majority of situations, where the parents do not show much interest in their daughter's school life and try and restrict her if she wants to enter higher education.

For Muslim parents, whether peasant or urban in background, their daughter's education in Britain is fraught with conflict between the demands of the school system and the requirements of Islam. According to the Koran, for example, women and girls must always cover their arms and legs. This makes the wearing of school uniform difficult. To add to the confusion the old-fashioned but still prevalent school ethics dictate that girls in trousers are somehow 'rude'.

At least if there is a uniform a rule is seen to exist, but it is in schools where there is no uniform but where girls are prevented from wearing trousers that the greatest conflict can arise. Take the case of Essex Junior School in Newham described in *Spare Rib* issue 55:

At the beginning of the school year, Mr Bailey, the head teacher, would remind the staff about various rules at the school and he would also give us his view about clothes. He didn't want female teachers or pupils to wear trousers – the teachers because it is "unladylike and unprofessional" and the girls for "reasons of hygiene", says Cathy Pemberton, an ex-teacher from Essex Junior School in Newham. The girls are mainly Asians (Muslims and Sikhs). If they come in trousers they are warned or made to take them off. Wearing trousers is more than a fashion choice for them, it is a religious requirement. So they spend their time changing into and out of trousers – at assembly, at every playtime, at lunchtime and when they go home. Parents who questioned what appears to be an unwritten regulation have been told in each case that they are the only ones not co-operating . . . Edward Bailey commented 'There is no rule against girls' wearing trousers and anyone who says there is is guilty of libel.' Meanwhile more religious Muslim parents are saying that the answer to it all is single sex schools.

In Bradford it was just such issues which gave impetus to the demand for single sex schools. Orthodox Muslim parents felt that the schools were making an almost deliberate attempt to obstruct them in their efforts to bring up their daughters as Muslims. While local authorities and Muslim groups in Bradford squabbled over the rights and wrongs of the matter, and the press reported with relish the 'grotesque' attitudes of Muslim parents, no one really asked the daughters what they thought about it. But on the specific question of 'showing' one's legs, after talking to Muslim girls in Bradford and London I feel convinced that they share the views of their parents. Dilip Hiro in his book *Black British, White British* looks briefly at the subject. He quotes a young Pakistani woman recalling her schooldays, when she had to change for swimming and showers: 'I was surprised at the English girls who simply used to stand there and change. They didn't seem to be embarrassed, whereas I used to try and hide everything and felt conscious of myself.' According to Hiro, 'the explanation of this difference of attitudes lies in the variation between the home environment of the Asian and English children. Mehtab, for instance, had never seen her mother or father sunbathing in the back garden. Nor had she ever seen her mother expose her breasts or even legs, at home. She had therefore grown up subconsciously feeling that nakedness was undesirable, even immoral.'

When I asked a Pakistani woman in her forties about this interpretation, she said:

It is true but it is not the full reason. You can say religion forbids us to show our legs. You can say we are not used to it because our parents never sunbathed. But deeper than all this are the values of our society. You see we think that for a woman *Sharam* (shame or shyness) itself is honour. It can be a woman's pride because it reflects her purity and sensitiveness.

In a sense *Sharam* is the complement of *Izzat*. It is common in one form or another to all Indo-Pakistani cultures. Its effects can vary from never looking a man in the eye or never arguing with a man, to wearing a *Burkha*. Few women brought up in India can truthfully say that they have never felt *Sharam*. For the unwary it is a feeling as infectious as embarrassment or flirtatiousness. It can be very enjoyable, amusing and romantic (because it means that a relationship with a man must deepen through glances, smiles and phrases with hidden meanings). But inevitably it robs women of their strength and power and cramps their personality.

Since *Sharam* in its extreme Muslim form is the antithesis of openness and frankness, to preserve it, no information about the body should be openly available to a woman. This has brought Islam once again into direct confrontation with the British school system. Most of the Pakistani mothers I asked were against sex education in school. Rifat, a woman in her late thirties with an urban background in Pakistan, told me:

I don't think they should learn about these things at such an early age. In Pakistan, when girls go to school or college, they learn about it from their friends. Those who don't learn that way? Well, they find out after marriage. But here my fourteen-year-old daughter was shown a film about it in school. She was shocked, stunned by it all. She was deeply embarrassed and ashamed. For a woman *Sharam* is such a precious quality . . . Now eight or nine-year-olds are being taught about periods in schools. For us it was when we finally got a period that we learned about it. Our mothers explained. My daughter also didn't know about it till she had it in school. If you get to know about these things at an early age you lose your shame and shyness. You have all the knowledge, and all the choices are available, and the trouble is that with all this knowledge a child does not know what to do, how to make a decision.

Rifat's opinions were shared by many others, Hindu, Muslim and Sikh, but her family in Pakistan must have been exceptionally reticent about sex. Ruksana's comments about sex education in the joint family were more typical:

For a girl not to know about periods before she has them? That must be rather upsetting. In our family my cousins and I knew well beforehand because there were always slightly older sisters and cousins who told us . . . About sex? Yes, that too. I knew all about it in theory because I had a young *Bhabi* and she used to tell her friends about her experiences and I used to overhear (laughs). In our family we always learn from each other.

Once an Asian girl has finished school, whether she is Hindu, Muslim or Sikh, the threat or prospect of marriage begins to loom over her, casting a blight over her chances of further education. Once again Hindu girls from an urban background are most likely to study or at least to continue their courses after marriage, but for Muslim and Sikh girls higher education can rarely be achieved without a struggle. However good they might be as students, their families feel that marriage is infinitely preferable to a college career. This is not only because marriage is thought more important but because higher education is dangerous. In orthodox families, educated women are seen as destructive and potentially immoral, and an educated daughter is a source of scandal and potential family dishonour.

Jaswinder Kaur, a Sikh girl from such a family, described, in *Oppression of South Asian Women Vol 1, 1977*, what she had to go through to get to college:

I had a most successful career at school. I tried hard at school because I was most happy there – not at home where girls are not allowed to go out even with their female friends. My parents still don't know what course I am pursuing at a college of education. My headmaster and a teacher, after a long struggle, managed to convince my Papa that it was in my best interest to pursue such a training. Although he said a resigned 'Yes' to them, I was told by him I would never reach college. He threatened me with this throughout the examination period and until the day I actually left home. My eldest brother, who is quite 'westernised', took me to college. It was a fight but now that I am at college you can believe I am the happiest girl around here. Academic work has always meant freedom for me. It may be the only way in which I get what I want in my life. It is quite revolutionary that I have left home to attend college. The only reason a Sikh girl is allowed to do that is when she goes to her in-laws after marriage. Any scandal I may commit in my period out of my home would seriously affect my younger brothers and sisters. My father would clamp down on their education – their only means of freedom. Worst of all, my family would be ostracised socially [see chapter on 'Adolescence and Marriage'] from the Sikh community. How could I commit such an offence when I really do love my parents so much?

Muslim girls face the same harsh oppression. As Afshan Begum explains in her thesis 'In many cases parents expect that the girl will, whenever they demand, give up everything (e.g. a course in further education or training or a career) and submit without question to a marriage they have arranged for her . . . these hidden cases which no one gets to hear about are the real tragedies.' Those girls who attempt to escape are found in a few days. They have few outside contacts and white society is uncaring and often hostile towards them. Afshan Begum writes:

In one case I know of, two friends resolved to escape because they had heard their parents 'scheming' of such marriages in the near future. They were found after two days with the help of the police and brought home. On coming home, one, because of psychological stress and the consequences of not having resolved anything, preferred not to face the future – and therefore took an overdose. Ironically enough, on recovery her parents were gentler with her and began gradually to compromise to a certain extent, and now she is at a college of further education. The other girl was not so lucky, her attempted escape accelerated the plans for her marriage.

In yet another case quoted by Afshan, the girl went to ask the help of someone regarded as a community leader. This man took her back to her family without any mention, leave alone discussion, of the dilemma which confronted her. 'It seems,' writes Afshan 'that these people as well as the parents refuse to acknowledge that a problem of this nature exists.' The subject itself is taboo in many Muslim families, perhaps because Muslim parents regard it (as do the white media) as a choice between two life styles– one Asian and one British. But Afshan says the problem is not that, but one of how to keep one life style without rejecting the other, or, as Meena, the girl from Acton put it 'I never regard myself as English. I am an Indian in every way. It is just that I want to be free.'

VI
Adolescence and Marriage
'Izzat is easily hurt'

If you've been out with a bloke, say a famous bloke of Southall
like M—— everybody knows you've been out with him because
that guy is going to go and boast to his friends that he's been out
with this girl and he's done this to her and that to her. Even if he
hasn't, he'll boast about it. Then they get the girl's name bad.
That's why girls try and keep it quiet when they're going out with a
bloke, because they don't want any one to know. It's quite
different for boys, they can get away with it. Their names can't
ever get spoilt.

Sofia, who told me this, is a Muslim girl of nineteen. She has a
stylish and confident way of speaking. She wears quite a lot of
make-up, has an 'Indian film star' hairstyle and, like most Muslim
girls, usually wears trousers. The idea that a girl's reputation is
important is almost universal, but for Asian girls it is not just
important; 'reputation' is the bane of their lives from adolescence
to the early years of their marriage. It controls everything they do
and adds a very tangible danger to any unconventional action.

   In conversations I had with Asian girls from all language
groups and religions, in all parts of Britain 'reputation' came up
all the time. Girls as young as twelve, for example, told me that
'girls want to go out with boys but they are afraid to because of the
reputation they'll get. If other people in society find out, they'll
talk about it, and then you and your parents get a bad name.
When the time comes for you to get married, you can't because
people think you are really disgusting.' Even having friends, male
or female, who 'have been seen on the streets, smoking, drinking or
mucking about' can get to the ears of this community and mean
disgrace. Meena, a Gujerati Hindu girl of sixteen, told me:

My parents say 'We don't want you to go around with so and so',
say an English girl if she's been seen smoking. I can argue with
them, saying it's my life. I want to choose the people I go out with
but they say no — and 'what will the neighbours think if they see
you walking with them.' It's not really the neighbours. Both our

neighbours are English so they don't really care. But your parents have Indian friends and if they see you they talk about you. They like gossiping, and then there's your uncles and aunts; if they see you, you lose your reputation and it's a disgrace to your family.

Reputation is a tremendous, conservative force, controlling, to differing extents, everyone in Asian societies. It is related directly to male pride or *Izzat*. Disgracing your family means in effect hurting the Izzat of your father or brothers, and Izzat can be easily hurt, even destroyed. A girl's family can be disgraced if she wears halter-necks or other revealing clothes, if she goes out with boys or with girls who are in any way immodest. Some girls who have orthodox families can even bring disgrace on them by going out with English or West Indian girls, because 'their way of life is completely different from ours and our parents think we might adopt their ways'. Even choosing a career is seen to have hidden pitfalls; careers other than teaching, medicine or nursing are regarded, particularly by Muslim families, as potentially dangerous.

Yet in spite of all these rules, or perhaps because of them, many girls do do that risky and wicked thing, they go out with boys. In two West London colleges groups of Asian girls I spoke to told me that about half of them went out or had been out with boys. But the proportion who did so varied according to what age they had come to Britain and also with their religion: Muslim girls had the least freedom.

Given all the risks of going out why did they do it? Some said 'for kicks' or 'because it is supposed to be wrong'. Others said they wanted to have the freedom which English girls had. One sixteen-year-old Gujerati girl told me of the pressures to be westernised:

In school I was in a group of Indian girls who went out with boys. I didn't want to but they'd try and make me. They thought it was a status thing – at the same time I don't know if they really knew why they were doing it. They thought it was wrong, so perhaps they wanted to know what doing something wrong was like. They liked to talk about it, show off much more than English girls. They'd say to me 'Oh go on, go out with that boy, he likes you.' I'd say 'I don't want to, my parents don't want me to and not only that, I myself don't want to.' They'd say, 'Go on, please, it makes us Indians look so odd if you don't'.

In general, the girls who do go out do so very tentatively. Their demands are small. They want freedom but only a little. It is almost as though they are playing at being free. They know the barriers around them and they only want room to manoeuvre within these barriers. They certainly don't want a real relationship with a boy, in fact they do their best to avoid it. 'It is because of my parents,' Meena told me. 'Everything I do is for them, they are the centre of my life. If I found I was getting too close to a boy I'd leave him – stay away from him.' Nirmal, a Sikh girl, said:

You can't have a proper relationship with a boy in case it got too serious. You just have to break it off if it gets like that. That's why mostly we don't go out with Asians but with Cypriots and other Europeans – they too have arranged marriages and they don't want a serious relationship. We could go out with Asians but we prefer not to because with an Asian boy there is usually more trouble. You can't break it off easily and if he's your kind of Asian (Gujerati or Punjabi), his parents might find out and then your parents might find out.

The worlds of home and school must be kept strictly apart because, as Nirmal explained: 'Apart from anything else you are two people, you see. In front of your parents you are different and outside you are different. When I am at home I am ever so quiet. But when I am here (in college) people might think I am a loudmouth. So I have two faces.' When she got married which face would she keep for her husband? 'The one I keep for my family. I don't really believe in arranged marriage but I'll go through with it for my culture.'

But most girls I spoke to told me not only that they were going to have arranged marriages but that they 'believed' in them. They gave me a variety of reasons. Some of these were obviously their parents' opinions, such as 'my parents have more experience, they are more likely to choose the right person' or that popular Indian fallacy 'There is more success in arranged marriage than in love marriage because there are more divorces in love marriage.' Others were more deeply thought out reasons such as 'If you had a love marriage and it failed you would have a divorce and then you would be likely to be rejected by the community. You would have nowhere to go' or 'You couldn't go back to your parents' home if you had a love marriage. You would have nowhere to go if your husband left you.'

Even girls as young as twelve or thirteen realised the implications of a love marriage – that you alone and not your family would be responsible for its success or failure; and that you were putting yourself first, before your culture, your community and even your parents, that you were placing your parents at risk because it is they who would be disgraced. And in doing all this, in becoming free you might lose the love and support in which you have grown up. To break out of the family's arm-lock you also have to cast off its embrace.

However, most girls I spoke to stressed that arranged marriage was not the tyrannical system it was made out to be. Many of them told me to say so in my book, because the publicity it receives, they told me, is always in terms of girls being forced, parents being cruel. In reality, they said, it is much less traumatic, much more 'semi-arranged'. The parents choose someone, invariably of the right background, religion and caste. The girl is asked if she approves and if she does they get engaged. Sometimes they get to know each other better before they finally get married. Geeta, a nineteen-year-old girl whose mother was trying to arrange a marriage for her, told me 'If my mum shows me a boy and I refuse, she does not mind. She asks me the reason and I tell her. If it is not my cup of tea I don't have it, and that's the case with most girls.'

The widely-publicised arranged marriages forced on girls brought up in Britain to boys from India or Pakistan are in fact a dwindling minority. Most people, parents and children, disapprove of them. Sofia, for example, told me:

Such marriages can't be expected to work in most cases. Our parents had typical arranged marriages, not seeing their fiancées before marriage. They accepted it because they were brought up in a typical Indian culture and society. But we have been brought up in England. We see things differently. Arranged marriages like that aren't right for us. But I do think that arranged marriage is right when the girl has a chance to see the boy and say whether she like him or not. What happens now is that people get engaged. After you are engaged it takes a year or so to make the dowry. During that period you do get to know the person. That's how it happened with my sister. She had the engagement and the civil marriage. After they had known each other for a year they had the *Nikka* (Muslim marriage). In that period they were allowed to go out together but usually I'd go with them. They did go out by themselves but they preferred going out with someone because they didn't want any talk. Because you know how people talk.

(The arrangement Sofia describes is similar to marriage arrangements in upper-class urban families in India; in fact when Asians from a peasant background, settled in Britain, return to India or Pakistan, they do have more money than they had before and they are considered to have gone up in class and status.)

Meena, a Hindu, told me of her sister's engagement: 'after they got engaged they developed a really good relationship. They are not thinking of getting married for a long time but they have a boyfriend-girlfriend relationship; it's just that they have the title of fiancées.'

Is it progress towards liberation when marriages are only 'semi-arranged' and not arranged? In the 'improved' set-up you are still coerced but you are allowed the dignity of pretending that you are doing it of your own free will. Underneath it all the system remains the same. There is freedom to say no to one or two boys of the right background chosen by your parents, but no girl can be allowed to go on refusing for ever, and certainly no girl is allowed to object to the principle of it. What if a girl fell in love with someone and wanted to marry him, I asked? This, most of the girls agreed, would be a very unwise thing to do, probably with most unpleasant consequences. 'If the boy was of the girl's religion' said Sofia 'she'd probably stand a chance. She should tell her parents that there was this bloke she wanted to marry and he was of her religion.' What happens if he isn't her religion or caste? 'That's her tough luck,' she said. 'One should try not to get into that situation. It's just going to create problems for the girl and her family.'

And yet many girls I spoke to had got themselves into this situation. Their stories were bitter, and often even those who had eloped successfully were sad. The attitudes they had faced in their families were age-old ones – always rigid and immovable, sometimes brutal. Manjula is a Hindu Gujerati girl of nineteen from North London. Her story is almost a classic one, differing only in minor details from those of hundreds of other Asian girls from all parts of Britain.

Manjula fell in love with a boy she met at a school dance. She was fourteen at the time and he was three years older. Like her he is a Gujerati but, while she is a Brahmin, he is of the Jetwa caste. Since going out together openly was not possible they would go to the library and sit there and chat. Occasionally they went to the pictures but that was difficult because she had to be home by

9.30 p.m. This went on for four years; then Manjula left college and got a job as a computer operator. Her boyfriend became an accountant. Finally Manjula told her mother that she had a boyfriend and that she wanted to marry him. This is what she told me happened:

Her reaction was really frightening. She began to cry. She said I had disgraced the family, that I must promise never to see him again or she'd kill herself. I tried and tried to explain how I felt but she didn't want to know. She kept saying 'You have disgraced us and degraded yourself! He is of a lower caste! You must stop seeing him!' She made me promise never to see him again. Because of my parents we broke up twice but we couldn't stay apart. Soon after, my mother went to India for a visit. When she came back she said 'I have found a nice guy for you.' I said 'I don't want to marry him, I want to marry my boyfriend.'
    After that the conflict and distrust became unbearable. My parents, really in that period they were terrible. They wouldn't let me go out even for shopping. I used to go to college; when I came back from my classes they wouldn't let me go anywhere, even if it was just round the corner to the shop. They would say 'you are going to telephone him, we know.' That lasted nearly two years . . . My boyfriend never used to force me to come out, never. He was just scared that I wouldn't marry him in the end.
    If I had married someone else, it would have been – Oh, I don't know if I would have survived, or what. Especially because I had known him and loved him for six years. Two years of that time I tried to make my parents change their minds. I couldn't. I tried to argue, I cried and cried, nearly every mealtime it was like that. I'd sit there arguing. Often I'd leave my dinner and go upstairs and cry and cry. I got so depressed. They would say 'Don't you see you'll spoil our name. Don't you care for your parents? What kind of girl are you, we brought you up and you don't care for us.' I tried my best to convince them, to change them about this. But I don't think they could change. I don't think my mum could ever change.

In the end Manjula ran away — 'My boyfriend told his mum. She didn't mind (maybe because they are of a lower caste). We fixed a date and when the day came, instead of going to work I came here (her parents-in-law's house), got dressed and then we got married at the registry office.'
    Manjula is luckier than many girls; at least her elopement went

off smoothly and her husband's parents with whom the couple live have accepted her completely. But her own parents have not forgiven her. They have told her that as far as they are concerned she is dead. Her mother-in-law approached them hoping for a reconciliation, but, was rejected. As for her brother, Manjula says:

He is only one year older than me but he does not understand me. He doesn't want to know me. He says 'She has hurt my parents, I don't want to know her. For me my sister is dead. I don't want to see her till the day I die.' My mum gets sick quite a lot now. She's got high blood pressure. But if anything happens to my mum or my father, my brother says – 'that's because Manju left home.' He blames everything on me . . . sometimes I feel so guilty, because I did love my parents. There were so many good times before all this happened. On Saturdays we'd go shopping with my dad. They told me they'd give anything, anything at all if I got married to the boy they chose.

Why, why do parents like Manjula's behave so unreasonably? Often enough the British press has treated us to melodramatic accounts of girls running away from brutal parents but no reason is ever given for these parents' behaviour. Everything is explained away in terms of 'culture'. But parents have a much more easily understandable reason for their action – fear. Fear not of God but of the deeply conservative institutions within Asian societies. In *The Oppression Of South Asian Women*, Vol I, Jaswinder Kaur, a Sikh girl, describes the treatment received by Asian girls who are in any way unconventional:

Indian teenagers like myself are regarded as outcasts and their parents forced by gossip and influences within the structures of society to supervise their children more strictly. The parents are dictated to by these gossips, who may happen to hold a higher rank in the society.

A girl wanting to marry outside her religion or even caste is for parents a dire emergency. They must stop her, they feel, at all costs – by locking her up, beating her, sending her back to India, even in some cases by killing her, otherwise they'll suffer all their lives. They will be ostracised, no one will marry their other children, if they ever go to Asian gatherings they'll be insulted and treated with contempt, even their relations may not receive them. If the girl can't be prevented from marrying a man of her own choice the parents might be able to escape blame if they cut her off completely. The constant righteous gossip, which is a characteristic of all Asian communities, ensures that parents don't forget their 'duties'.

If marrying out of your caste is considered so drastically wrong, it can be imagined how 'running off' with a West Indian or an Englishman is seen; and yet it seems to be endemic among Gujerati girls in some parts of Britain. For example, of a group of seven teenage girls who discussed their lives and attitudes with me, five had relations or close friends who had done just this. They told me about it with disapproval and relish: a thirteen-year-old girl said:

My aunt ran away with a coloured bloke. He had three kids and a divorce from his first wife. Afterwards my aunt asked her mum if she could come back to them but her mum didn't agree. But when her dad came he said he would take her back. I don't know exactly what happened next but I think the whole family had a talk. My mum and dad didn't think she should be taken back but her mum and dad did, so she came back, and they gave her wedding presents! Everyone gave her wedding presents! And the coloured man kept his kids!

Usha (twelve) said:

My cousin she had children by a coloured person. She used to live in Africa before now she lives in Brent. She got married to an Indian person and had three children by him and then she had two children by this coloured person. I mean I'd have thought one would have been enough but she had two. I don't know whether her husband knows about the affair.

Geeta told me:

My cousin ran off with a white man who was married with children. She says she wasn't treated well by her parents and that is true, but that doesn't mean you run off with a white man . . . She ran away last summer; at first her parents didn't want to know her, they said they had forgotten all about her. But in four or five months they changed. Now she goes to their house every two or three days and they are ready to accept her any time she goes. I don't think they should because it is a disgusting thing to do to run off with a white man who is married with children.

Was it disgusting because he had children? 'Not because he had children but because he had a wife. The children are going to cry, or they might if they like their father. But what about his wife?'

Would her reaction have been the same if the man had been Asian? 'Yes, if he had been married it would have been the same. Although of course I wouldn't really like her to go with a white man even if he wasn't married. I am not colour prejudiced but I think for marriage there should be prejudice.'

The majority of girls I spoke to were like Geeta – against mixed marriages, not because there was anything wrong with them but because they felt such marriages hadn't a chance. Niru, a girl of fourteen told me 'I think you should marry in your own community. Because if you marry a white or coloured person, eventually, in time he is going to chuck you. I have known girls who have run off with white or coloured men – it may take some time, a year, a year and a half, two years then he goes off with another girl and you are left stranded.'

'White people,' I was told 'still have boyfriends and girlfriends after they are married. On the whole even after marriage they have the freedom to go anywhere and meet anyone. That way it is different for Asians.'

. What would life be like if they themselves fell in love with a white man and married him? Geeta spoke for the girls in the group:

If we married white men our lives would be changed completely. It is difficult to imagine how great the change would be. I may have to give everything up, everything that I am used to, like eating with my fingers or dressing the way I want to . . . And white people wouldn't like it that a white man has to marry an Indian girl. The white man would be made to feel degraded even if he didn't feel that way to start with.

Only one girl, a Sikh from Glasgow, had anything positive to say about mixed marriages. She pointed out that they often succeeded, and when they didn't it was not so much because of racial difference but because the families of the husband and wife, instead of supporting the couple, did everything to destroy their marriage. She told me of a young Scotsman, a friend of her father's, who had wanted very much to marry an Indian girl. Her father, obviously a man with flair and imagination, had arranged a marriage between this Scotsman and his own niece who at that time lived in India. He wrote to the girl's parents describing the prospective husband and asking whether they would insist on refusing this suitor just because he was not a Punjabi. Apparently the family had no answer to this. Just in case there was any gossip in their community in Delhi, the marriage was performed in Glasgow. The couple, who have the support of both families, have lived happily ever since.

These opinions about the destructive influence of disapproving families fit in well with what older Asian women married to Englishmen told me about their lives. One woman in her thirties had this to say about her relationship with her husband's family.

My husband comes from a middle-class English family. In marrying him I have had to live apart from my parents, who are in India, but I have not had to give them up, I visit them every two or three years. I have not really changed my outlook since I got married nor have I changed the way I dress or my way of life generally. The problems I have faced have been in fact comparatively mild. They are centred on the fact that while I have no family of my own in Britain, no relationship is possible with my in-laws either. At the same time my husband and I have kept on seeing them because my husband has very close bonds with them.

To start at the beginning, when my husband told his parents of my existence, my mother-in-law, he told me later, began to weep hysterically saying 'we had such hopes for you, now everything is spoilt!' My father-in-law's reaction was merely 'I don't really mind so long as she is not an African.' I did eventually get asked to the family home for Sunday lunch, where for the first time I experienced the ways of silent communication – of disapproval and guilt – which I now know are typical of English families. Over the first couple of years my mother-in-law's total rejection of me softened slightly. I reached a stage when she would accept me but only on the basis of a stereotype she had in her mind of Indian women, which was in no way connected with my own personality. I was expected, for example, to be submissive, incapable and undesiring of a career and, more than anything else, honoured to be a member of an English family such as hers. My father-in-law was the family expert on India. He had been there briefly in his army days and 'knew all there is to know' about the place. His attitude was heavily colonial.

Sometimes at larger family gatherings the older men would cluster round me presumably because being black I was assumed to be sexy. Their wives meanwhile looked on with dark disapproval. Occasionally when I met my mother-in-law on her own I felt that I was about to make real contact with her. But it never lasted more than a few moments; back in the bosom of the family she would revert to her usual distant self. Now after many years of this 'relationship' remaining unchanged, I have just copped out and stopped seeing my parents-in-law, leaving my husband to shoulder alone the heavy burden of guilt. Why he should feel guilty nobody, not even he, knows – maybe it is because he has ceased to care for his parents as much as he thinks he should. The decision that I should stop seeing his family was one my husband and I took together because we both feel that our marriage would be safer outside the guilt-ridden arena of his family.

How do Asian boys feel about arranged marriages? The cool, hip, westernised boys one sees in Southall, Birmingham and Sheffield, how do they feel about marrying girls they have seen only briefly or, as in many cases, girls they have never seen before from the remote villages of India and Pakistan? (Many more men than women settled in Britain marry spouses directly from the Indian sub-continent.) On the whole these boys, many of whom seem to almost radiate machismo, are surprisingly docile when it comes to arranged marriage. It is a minority who refuse; of these, a small number run away from home, the rest are bullied and threatened into marriage. A Muslim boy, for example, told me that he had initially refused to go home and have an arranged marriage but had given in when his father threatened to divorce his mother if he didn't marry. The father's reasons were the familiar ones – firstly Mohammed had been seen going out with English girls, and marriage, he thought, would put an end to that and the accompanying fear of 'disgrace', and secondly he wanted to forge stronger links with the girl's family. So the young couple got married in India and shortly after came to settle in Britain. Were they happy? 'We have very little in common,' said Mohammed 'I still do the things I liked doing before marriage, like going drinking with my mates and going to discos. My wife stays home, she doesn't speak English and doesn't know anything about life in England.'

What did they have in common? Only that they were distant cousins; they both told me about the days of their early childhood, carefree days spent in an Indian village. Would these shared experiences be enough for a future in a fraught joint family set-up in Stoke Newington? The vast majority of boys I spoke to accepted arranged marriage with equanimity. They were fully aware that as sons they were at the centre of the family. Marriage would hardly change their lives or the balance of their emotional relationships. It would mean that they would bring home not only a wife, a new servant for the joint family, but (in the case of Hindus and Sikhs) a large dowry. It is easy not to rebel against present tyranny when you are assured of a privileged position in the future. Only a tiny minority of boys were against arranged marriage for everything it symbolised about the enslavement and oppression of women; these men, often working-class boys who had done well academically, suffered acute emotional isolation; they were revolted by the system and often ended up unable to communicate at all with older women and men in the Asian community.

In previous chapters I have described how the upbringing of boys, from the moment of birth onwards, serves to nurture the male ego. When it comes to marriage, especially among Hindus and Sikhs, the dowry a girl brings symbolises not only her father's ability to pay but the amount her bridegroom is worth in terms of status and ego. The majority of young men I spoke to said that they would accept not only an arranged marriage but a dowry as well. In the Gujerati Hindu communities in Britain marriage without a dowry is unusual. Sums between £500 and £2000 are normal. Older women I spoke to were sometimes against the dowry system but powerless to change it. One Gujerati Hindu woman in her forties, mother of two sons, told me:

In India it (the dowry) was in rupees, in Africa in shillings, here it is pounds. In fact the dowry is one reason why some girls are encouraged to work by their parents, because their earnings can contribute to it. In some cases the dowry is made up entirely of the girl's earnings. Nowadays the boy's parents sometimes mockingly ask 'How much has your daughter earned and put away on the side.' That's why the younger generation are losing faith in their parents and in the Asian society. Add to this the younger generation's ignorance of old customs – what is it leading to – the breaking up of this society with young people leaving it, rejecting it ... If a boy is from a good family and well-educated, his parents think they can demand as much as they have invested in the boy.

Then there is the question of *Khandan* (position in the community). Sometimes the bridegroom's parents think the girl is coming to a home of high *Khandan* so I should get something for it. The bride's father's attitude may be – their *Khandan* is not very high, in fact it is lower than ours so why should I pay a lot. Of course, not every marriage involves a dowry but among Patels the majority do. Some parents may give because they want to, that's different. But the trouble is that people like to copy and outdo each other and it is taken out on the girl. She may be asked by her parents-in-law why she hasn't brought a bigger dowry. And apart from the actual dowry there is the jewellery. There is the custom that the jewellery must be displayed. When people come to see the bride they come to see the jewellery too, in theory to celebrate the generosity of the parents. Unfortunately what it amounts to is pure materialism, people showing off what they have got.

Dowry has long been recognised as one of the evils of Indian society. For nearly a hundred years progressives in India have campaigned against it but have achieved very little. In the 1890s Girish Ghosh, a Bengali author, wrote a play 'Balidan' (or Sacrifice) which described the effects of the dowry system on a middle-class family; and things have changed only marginally since then. The family consists of father, mother, three daughters and a son. The father sells his wife's jewellery, and mortgages his house to pay the dowry for Kiran, the eldest daughter. The bridegroom is a good-for-nothing, his mother is vicious. The girl is beaten and insulted. Her parents are abused. Her husband humiliates her because she is dark skinned. One day they send her to her father's house, forbidding her to return till her father pays more money. There she continues to live. Her mother is sympathetic but her father seldom is. He is a bitter man plagued by the thought of the other two daughters' marriages. The second girl, Hiran, can't be given a dowry because the family have nothing more to sell, but she has to be married. Finally when she is fifteen a man is found who will take her without a dowry. He is nearly seventy years old and has two sons nearly her father's age. In a few years' time he dies and his two sons throw Hiran out. She is penniless and a widow – she too comes back to her father's house. It is too much for her father; he has had to sell his house and stop sending his son to school because he cannot afford the school fees. When Hiran arrives he loses all control and says 'Having devoured your husband you have come home; here too you must eat well. Go and bring the ashes out of the oven so we can all eat them . . . You were born at an auspicious moment, that is why you bring good fortune wherever you go.' Hiran leaves, crying, and drowns herself in the pond. Her father loses his mind and dies soon after.

The play highlighted firstly the powerlessness of widows and the fact they had no right to their husband's property (legal reforms have now changed this in India), and secondly the helplessness of parents in the face of the dowry system.

In India the dowry system remains as strong as ever; no effective legislation against it is possible. Why have all campaigns against the dowry system failed in India? Perhaps it is because of the economic power distribution in Indian families. Women are powerless because they do not earn a wage and have no real control over money. If this argument is correct, then over the next ten years or so dowry taking and giving will fade out in the Gujerati communities in Britain. But against this argument is the fact that among Patels dowries are still exorbitant and increasingly a girl's earnings are simply used to augment her dowry. In addition, since dowry is a reflection of the status of the bridegroom, the insecurity felt by the Patels who have come to Britain as refugees is likely to mean that dowries will be high for many years to come, thus acting as a palliative for battered egos. Whatever the future of the dowry system, the upbringing of adolescent girls in Britain is at present still overshadowed by the economic and psychological preparation for marriage. Money must be collected for a dowry and at the same time a girl must be kept in her place because in time she'll become somebody's daughter-in-law. Geeta explained it to me:

My mum treats my brothers better than the way she treats me. She's stricter with me because she thinks when I get married I'll be going away to another family. I have to have manners, proper manners. Otherwise they'll say she is this person's daughter and look at the way she behaves. So there should be hardly any answering back. You should quietly do the housework. Boys can get away with arguing. They'll be staying on in their parent's home so there'll be no outsider who will criticise them.

Of course not all families are so orthodox. In many, boys and girls do argue with their parents. In a few families housework is shared and opinions readily given. But Geeta's explanation is a description of the original basis from which new life styles have been devised – not on the basis of principle, but for convenience. These life styles may seem different, but in fact are very similar in ideology.

The arranged marriage system has often been criticised in England because the couple don't meet beforehand, because it involves having sex with a man or woman with whom one has no previous emotional relationship, because it means that parents decide the future of their grown up children. But these are minor inconveniences – small matters of style on the surface which can be, and are being, changed. Increasingly, for example, the future husband and wife do meet and go out together before they marry. But what is wrong with arranged marriage is far more fundamental – that it is an essential part of the gigantic and oppressive framework, the joint family, which has for so many generations kept women in subjugation. Previous chapters have shown that the joint family is no happy commune made up of equal partners. It is an hierarchy economically and in terms of power, one to which the oppression of women is basic. Right at the bottom of the hierarchy is the new bride.

A Gujerati girl, Pravina, told me what being on this lowest rung can mean to a girl living in Britain:

I came to Britain in 1970 when I was eighteen. I had done my 'O' levels in East Africa. When I came here I worked in a factory for some months. When I had saved enough money I took a course as a punch-card operator and got a job. I was very happy working and I didn't want to marry at all. If anything I would have preferred a love marriage, a marriage of my own free will, but my brothers insisted on my meeting a boy and his family. I must say when I met him I liked him. He was very good looking and pleasant. But his family – even then I did not like them. He and I talked for fifteen or twenty minutes in a separate room. But I refused to get married on the basis of that so it was decided that in the next three months we would get to know one another and then get married. He used to come to my house almost every day, we used to go out together. We were happy in those days. But even at that stage I used to tell him that I didn't like his family. He used to reassure me and promise that if things got bad we would not have to live with his family.

On the day of our marriage his family brought three or four hundred guests to eat at the reception. We had prepared a wonderful meal but it was just slightly less than they had wanted and so my in-laws were displeased. Among our community (Jains) the girl's family doesn't give a dowry as such, but the wedding cost my family £2000, that included expensive saris for twenty or thirty of my husband's relatives, food for the guests, cost of booking the hall, jewellery for me and, of course, a gold watch for my husband. Even then my husband's family were not satisfied. When I went back home after the wedding everyone seemed to be in mourning. I don't know why they were crying. I asked many times but never found out.

That day, the wedding day, my husband also became upset; his sisters and sisters-in-law were weeping. In the evening three or four male relations of his came and took him out. They made him drink a lot. I went upstairs to our room and waited for him. I didn't know he had gone drinking. When he returned he lay down on top of the bed and asked me to go and put my nightdress on. There was a small room adjoining our bedroom, a sort of dressing room. I went there to change. When I came back he had gone downstairs. But he soon returned, bringing his two sisters-in-law. Then he began to cry and the two sisters-in-law began to cry as well. The three of them sat on the bed crying. My husband laid his head on their laps and wept. I just stood there looking at them. I couldn't understand anything. Then my husband said to me 'I have ruined your life.' He began to beg me to forgive him and also not to run away, because he said, that would spoil his name – if I ran away on the first night. He said to me again and again 'My home is no good, my family are no good but don't leave me, please don't leave me.'

The next day he had recovered and my life in his house started. It was a large house and there were thirteen people in it – my parents-in-law, who were quite old, my grandmother-in-law who was very old, my husband's eldest brother and his wife and children and his fourth brother and his wife and children. (The second and third brothers and their wives had left because they couldn't stand it and my husband was the fifth.)

My husband's eldest sister-in-law – she was terrible. She was in her forties. She had got married at eighteen in Kenya when her brothers-in-law were children. She said she had brought them up and was responsible for them.

Before marriage my husband and I used to go out together to films and shows; after marriage all that stopped. He told me we couldn't go out together, *Bhabi* (sister-in-law) would not like it. She didn't like to see a couple enjoying themselves together because she had never gone out or enjoyed herself with her husband. She never even sat with him or talked to him. She even resented my going out to work; she'd say 'You go to work and work in comfort. I stay home and slave away.'

The first Friday my husband's brother said 'Where's your pay?' I told them that I was paid monthly but they wouldn't believe it. I was prepared to give all my salary to my husband but his *Bhabi* said 'I am the oldest daughter-in-law so I must keep all the money.' My husband forced me to give it to her. On my pay day they asked me to go to the bank and bring my full salary in. But when I went to the bank they said it hadn't been paid in yet. I explained that to my husband but he refused to understand. He said 'No, that won't do. Go and get it now and give it to *Bhabi*.' The first month they kept my entire salary. I had to beg my husband's elder brother for my travelling expenses.

Once I came home from work I was a prisoner. *Bhabi* didn't like me to go out, even to throw the rubbish in the bin. She would do it herself with her sari pulled down over her head. They said I was dirty because although I am a strict vegetarian they said that they knew I always ate meat at work. Because of that they wouldn't let me do the cooking, but I had to do all the cleaning right till midnight. Even if I thought I had finished, *Bhabi* would find something else.

There were many small things they wanted me to do like plastering down my hair with oil or wearing an ornament in my nose. I refused to do these things because I don't like them. Watching TV was forbidden although my father-in-law would sit watching TV all day. They would say 'The *Bahu* (daughter-in-law) must not sit and watch TV.' Then there was the food I had to eat; almost always it would be the previous day's chapattis – unheated. *Bhabi* would say 'I have made many sacrifices in my time, now you must make them.' I told my husband many times 'Come to the kitchen when I eat and see for yourself.' He never did. He never intervened.

Then my husband and I and my mother-in-law and father-in-law went to India on holiday. They went on a pilgrimage while my husband and I stayed on in Bombay. In that period we were happy, really happy and close. But when we got back it all began again. *Bhabi* couldn't bear to see us happy. If my husband had an evening at home, *Bhabi* would phone up his friends and ask them to come round and take him out. He'd go drinking usually. One day I said 'I'll not let you go. If you go I'll come with you.' He said 'No! You'll not go out! You'll remain with *Bhabi*.' In the next few weeks it was almost as though she wanted me tied to her. Wherever she went I had to go. To the bathroom or kitchen. She said 'You must wash my baby's nappies. You'll have to.' But I refused. She made a terrible scene.

One night when I was begging my husband not to go out and leave me, he pushed me out of the house. I went to my family's home and finally told my brother who had arranged my marriage what I had had to suffer. My mother I had already told but my brothers knew nothing about it. My brothers were not happy that I had come back to them but they allowed me to stay on. A few days later some friends of my husband's came to our house and asked me if I wanted a divorce or did I want to go back to my husband. Eventually I decided to try again. I went back to my husband's family for about a month. But things got steadily worse. In that period I gave up my job. I just couldn't concentrate or do any work and my boss kept threatening me. My English colleagues – well I tried to tell some of them what I was going through but they couldn't understand. They'd say why don't you just leave or why don't you find yourself a new boyfriend.

Then one day I had an appointment with the doctor. My husband had given me permission for that but when I got back he said he did not know where I had been. He told my father-in-law that I had been out with my boss. My father-in-law phoned my brother and said 'Take your sister away. We don't want her. She does no work and she's roaming with men all day.' My husband said 'Get out! Go now!.' He tried to push me out of the house but I got back in. My brother didn't come to fetch me because he thought if he did the fault would be pinned on him, and our family would get a bad name.

That night I got a fever. My head was blazing. I knew that in that house they would not allow me to sleep. I could bear it no longer so I came back to my brother's house. I decided I could stand the marriage no longer. I am trying to get a divorce and maintenance. They'll have to pay and that should teach them something. It has already come up in court and they have lost but they are trying to take it to a higher court.

In court my husband got upset. His family were not with him and he told the truth – that he and I had been happy but I had refused to obey his sister-in-law and do the housework so he had pushed me out of the house – that it was an Indian custom that a woman must obey and work for her husband's family, otherwise she must be got rid of.

VII
Sisters in Struggle

The women in this chapter are not typical of any sociological sample. They are not meant to be. But their struggles would find echoes and analogies in the lives of most Asian women in Britain. To see their lives with their own perspective, no added information is required.

Prabhaben: (a section of this interview appears in Chapter 3, 'Work Outside the Home')

I came to Britain from Nairobi in 1968. There I was a housewife. I used to do the housework and look after my children. It was such a wonderful life, the life of a boss – that life was so fine. I came here with my children ahead of my husband because he thought that if I didn't we might lose our right to enter Britain. At that time Raju was five months and the other one was two years old. I went to stay with my sister-in-law. But after fifteen days she and her husband found me a room elsewhere because they had no room in their own house. The landlord in the new place was an Italian; in a couple of weeks he turned us out. It was because I used to fry *Pooris* and they didn't like the smell. They just turned us out without notice.

Then my brother-in-law found us another room in Willesden Green. It was a tiny box room. I paid £5 a week for that but the people were very nice. All day my children and I would stay indoors in our room. I was scared in case they cried or made a noise and we were turned out. So we'd just stay in our house looking out of the window, waiting till it was time to feed my baby . . . And in Nairobi I had known such a life. The days seemed to be longer, the air sweeter than it can ever be in England. I had servants who did everything, I used to be proud . . . We had servants, here it is we who are the servants. I am a servant at home and at work.

We knew it was going to be hard. But we thought that if we worked hard we could make it. But this is what we have achieved with eight years work in Britain – a few rooms in a basement in an old house (in Newham). Anyway, from Willesden Green after my husband joined me we went to Birmingham, then to East London and finally here. In eight years we have moved nine times. After we came here I got a job at the laundry where I still work. It was like this, we lived in a place where the landlord used to harass us because he said that my babies made a lot of noise. Another tenant in the same house was an English girl who used to be very friendly and sympathetic to us. She was nice and she really liked my Raju. One day she said 'Come, I'll find you a job.' I said 'I don't know English and I have never worked before, I have no experience.' She said 'Come on, come and try.' Just imagine, she had never really spoken to me before but suddenly we were friends. I had learnt just a little English by then and one thing was that I was never shy about using it. She was a wages girl in the laundry and I got a job in the warehouse. And I must say the manager was good to me. He was an old Jewish man and he was kind. Once when I was ill he sent me a card and some flowers. On the card he had written 'As these flowers bloom so may you bloom and return to work because we are waiting.' But he was an old man and he died soon after I started work.

The new manager is not so nice. But you see there is no point in being sentimental, in this sort of world no one cares for anyone else, what they care for is your work and the old manager liked my work, that was all. Mind you, the pay was always bad. You asked me about discrimination, there is a colour bar that is for certain. First the pay. Indians get less. Oh yes, the whites get more. We get £28 a week whether we are operating heavy presses or sitting at a machine all day. The white women get £32. Upstairs where the machines are it is terribly hot. It is very difficult to work there. Almost all the workers there are women, there are only two men and they are pensioners. The women's salaries are very low, the pay in laundries is very poor, they can't afford to pay more, that is what they say. In many ways I am better off than the others. I work downstairs. Upstairs the women suffer, they really suffer. They don't speak English. That is why, perhaps, they are treated like this. They are paid low salaries and everything is worse for them, they have to face the insults of supervisors. These supervisors are all English women. The trouble is that in Britain our women are expected to behave like servants and we are not used to behaving like servants and we can't. But if we behave normally, like saying a few words to each other, the supervisors start shouting and harassing us. Or if they go to the toilet and take just a little longer. Of course, white women do that too but the supervisors don't notice them. They complain about us Indians to the manager. Our women suffer so much but usually they don't come out and complain. They don't know English but it is more than that. It is that all your life you have been soft and this treatment shocks and stuns you . . . But one or two of us have begun to speak up. Veena a Sikh girl who lives in Manor House, she is good. She doesn't take any rubbish and there are one or two others like her.

Sometimes I wish I could walk out and find another job but there isn't the time or energy to try, and anyway jobs are not easy to find. At 7.30 every morning the bus comes to pick us up at various centres; we have to clock in at eight. At lunchtimes they stop the machines and we eat what we have brought – *Sabji* and *Roti*. The windows are kept open but of course it is still very hot, especially in summer. Some of the older women, they are so shattered at the end of the day, some say they have lost ten years of their lives. In ten years from now where shall I be? Not in this position I think. Some women can go on suffering but I am not good at it.

Shahida:

In the morning I get up at eight and get the food ready. If there is the littlest thing wrong my husband is angry. If it is a cup of tea – if there is perhaps just a little bit less milk than he would like, he gets so angry. He leaves the cup on the table saying 'This is no good' and leaves the house. Tell me then how I burn! I work so hard and as I do it I remember and I am burning. I can cry, but what is the use, what support shall I get – from whom?

That is how it is for Asian women. The same story of a rotten life. Maybe one in a hundred is happy.

Yesterday a woman had come, a Pakistani: her husband has kept a white woman. He doesn't give his wife food or money – not enough anyway. If she complains he beats her cruelly. Is that a life worth living? She has no friend or support, no one except God. These white women have destroyed several homes. They are young white girls. For our men, we, their wives have only one purpose – as slaves. These girls provide other things. Five or six women I know have suffered like this. In the end the white girls leave, it never lasts. But our women are destroyed by sorrow and really they have no one who they can tell, no one who wants to hear.

I spend the morning cooking. At one o'clock lunch is over (every day he eats lunch at home). At 1.30 I take my daughter back to school. Tell me, doesn't one feel like taking a stroll sometimes – just once in a way? But if I do there are always remarks from him – 'You are always out roaming!' He doesn't realise, doesn't think – this is my wife, why should I hurt her so, break her spirit. She isn't well anyway and she is working all day.

Q. Why do you have to go out to work? Is it the money?

I don't know how much money he has. I don't know how much he gets or how much he had. After we were married in Pakistan he told me – you must stay with my mother, don't ask me for money.' I lived with my in-laws, my mother-in-law would bring me the vegetables and the meat. I would do all the cooking without ever handling any money, without ever having any money of my own. He used to obey his mother, only me he despised. After we got married, he came to England: he would return to Lahore every two or three years stay six months and then come back to England. After I finally came here to join him, he told me – 'I want to buy a house, you must try and find a job and make some money.' At that time I did not know any English at all, everything was new and bewildering, but anyway my brother-in-law found me a job in the laundry. I used to go at 7 am. and return at 5 pm. After that I had to do all the cooking.

Then I became pregnant; in that period I somehow managed to make my insurance stamps, seven of them. The way I made those stamps! Struggling all the time with my body, my weakness. After that I was at home for one year and since then it has been six years part-time at the laundry – 3.30 to 11.00 pm.

Soon after I went back to work after having Sweetie, my brother in Pakistan needed some help. He had to make his dowry to get married. My husband sent him some money but it was only a small amount – a thousand rupees. What is a thousand rupees – nothing. So my brother wrote to me that he wanted help. He was a student, a good student. (Now he has a good job). I told him not to worry. Then I got a job in the mornings. I'd leave Sweetie in school at 9 o'clock and then go to work, making jewellery. I'd finish there at twelve, pick up Sweetie from school and then come back, come back running to make the *Roti* in time for my husband's lunch. He'd eat and leave at 1.30. I'd start my cooking again, finish it and get to work by 2.30. I was ill with heart trouble.

But God gave me strength to help my brother. All those days I kept my laundry job as well. My husband never found out in all that time. At the end of a year I had made £500. I sent it to my brother. I said 'Here, take it, if I die, remember me.' My husband never found out because I was always at home in time for him with his supper ready. I ate my heart, my life to make that money. He was my youngest brother, he knew what I was going through, I had written to him. At that time, you see, my father had become poor and the money was needed.

These are the facts of my life, words from my gut. Tell them but keep my name a secret.

I was twenty when I married, now I am forty. Twenty years have passed. I have nothing to show for it. Sometimes I am filled with pain. I long to run away, escape, but where? And then there are my children, how can I leave them. They are very good children, they help me a lot. We women, we are so alone, our family, our parents, so, so, far away.

What my life was like before marriage, you are asking me sister? Well we lived as you know in a village area outside Lahore. In the morning I'd make breakfast for my younger brothers and sisters, then all of us girls would get together. We'd put the radio on and listen to the music programmes or we'd sit with our sewing or play skipping with our skipping ropes or hide and seek or other games. In the afternoon or evening, if we felt like helping around the house we did, otherwise my mother would cook our meal and we would sit and relax. In our family there were just the three of us children and my father and mother but our house was in a lane with other neighbours close by. Often I and my sister would spend all day in the corner house where our friends lived.

The men would go to work and the younger boys would go to school while we girls spent the day playing and frolicking. Life was so lovely. When the days of the Meena Bazaar approached I would be busy making *Dasuti* – I used to be quite talented at that. I was about fifteen then. The day of the Meena Bazaar, I was so happy, so proud. I set my hair, looked my best and stood there so proudly by my things. My mother had told me not to look at any boys because the family honour was at stake. I had told her I would never do that, but that I'd rather she threw me out of the house than try to control me . . . that was how it was, but after my marriage everything changed. I noticed how my husband was always angry. I told my mother about it. She said wait and see, he will change, he will soften. But he didn't. He used to mistreat me.

Q. Does he beat you?

Once he beat me in Pakistan but I dare him to beat me now. I'll give it back. It was when I went to the laundry I learnt about this because it was something women talked about – Asian women and even English. They said that the man cannot, has no right to, beat the woman. It is utterly wrong. Since then I have got wiser about this . . .

In the laundry all the workers now are Asian except for one Jamaican. In the past there were some white women. Now they have left for better jobs. I have to lift sheets, I catch them as they fall, folded. I have to put them in the cupboard in the right order depending on how they are labelled. It is a job standing all the time. It is a real strain. I get £18 a week for four hours a day. When I finish, my feet, the soles are like bricks and my arms aching. When I started work, at night it used to be agony till I fell asleep.

Our foreman is white. He is a swine. He makes us do ten minutes more every day. We are supposed to finish at 9.30 but he insists that we do ten minutes extra. Then he says that we steal things. He called Mrs B—(a community worker) and asked her to tell us in our language not to bring any bags to work. As it is they search our bags when we come in and when we leave. And to tell the truth the sheets are so thick it would be impossible to steal them in our bags. So it is humiliation just for the sake of it. That is what we told Mrs B but she only told us to work hard and to try to learn English. But that is not easy because there is no time. The laundry will allocate no time, all they can do is ask us to come one hour earlier. How can we, tell me how can we? There is never any time for anything. For example my husband is very religious, he has been on *Haj*; he says to me 'Why don't you read *Nimaz*?' It is true I don't, but when can I find time? I return home at 11 o'clock and then there is cleaning and tidying. It may be one in the morning before I get to bed. Tell me, how could I get up every day at six to read *Nimaz*? . . . Of course he gets up at five and reads all five Nimaz. He complains 'How will the children learn, what sort of an example are you setting them?' I just say 'May Allah forgive me, how can I live?' On Saturday and Sunday I work all day with the cleaning and washing. He starts with Nimaz, then he watches TV, reads Nimaz again then watches TV again, that's how the day passes. He never, ever does the housework. If I am ill he asks the children to do it.

It is not like this for all couples; for my parents it was different, my father never did what my mother did not want, my parents-in-law too were happy. It is a question of my ill-luck but I know that there are many others like me, many, many others. When Sweetie marries I'll ask her to bring someone she loves and who also loves her. And it is the same with my sons – when they marry I'll say, go now, you are free. You don't have to serve us. What's the use of your staying with a man who hurts his own wife? Only I will stay with him because I am his wife and I have nowhere to go.

Many people say white people are no good, their culture is no good. But I don't agree, their culture is good because if a man and woman are happy they can make their lives together, if not they can leave each other and marry again. At least they can enjoy their lives. Among us, how many are there who enjoy their lives? The question does not arise. All that matters is whether money keeps coming into the pocket. Only if a man wants to be happy and wants to enjoy his life with his woman, then she can live in happiness and joy . . . Life is so short soon it will be finished, the weeping of every day will be over.

Babli:

My mother was married when she was ten and my father was twenty-nine. He was a qualified engineer. He had studied and worked in Calcutta. His marriage was arranged by relatives. He had not even seen my mother before his marriage nor had he been told anything about her. After the marriage, when he saw my mother – how young she was – he was really angry. He said 'What am I expected to do? Take her away in my pocket?' Anyway two or three years after the marriage he took her to live with him in Murshidabad, a small town in India where he was working at the time. He taught her to read and write and she did the matric. exam and then trained in arts and crafts. My mother was very intelligent.

She was keen on music and my father too was a good singer. They were very happy together. But my father died when I was quite young. My mother was stricken with grief and shock. Soon after that we moved to the countryside and went to live in a village. My father, although he was an engineer, hadn't saved much money. The reason was mainly that he didn't take bribes. Anyway we were in a pretty helpless situation. All we had in our favour was that our mother was educated. It was thanks to that that we children eventually got our education. We were sent to school in Comilla and after that we went to college in Dacca. My mother

moved to P—, a small town in the district of Dacca. There she got
a job in the school teaching crafts. My mother was a teacher, and
hence middle-class but she was always close to the people of the
villages. When floods or storms hit the villages and cholera
started to spread we would go with the teams of workers to help,
give injections and so on. We learned all these things from my
mother.

In 1970 I was due to appear for my M.Sc exam in Dacca
University. I used to live with my uncle and his family in Dacca.
That year the country was in turmoil. The movement to oust
Ayub Khan was at its peak. Political unrest had overwhelmed
Dacca. As for me, my future was beginning to worry my mother.
You see, because I was doing an M.Sc, I was becoming less and
less marriageable. If a girl is doing a B.A., that's fine, she can get
married. But if she has finished a B.A. and is at the next stage,
then people think she is well on her way to getting a job and
becoming like a man. People think 'how can I bring such a girl
into my family as a *Bahu* (daughter-in-law)'. So that was what
was worrying my mother.

My brother, meanwhile, had passed his exams and come to
England for higher studies. When he went back for a holiday my
mother told him about her worries. He was the eldest, it was up to
him to find me a husband. He was only about twenty five but after
realising how my mother felt he began to regard it as a duty,
responsibility and worry of his own. At last he found a suitable
person; this person was in England. He was my brother's friend's
friend. He was good looking we were told, talked well and his
family in Dacca were certainly very well off. His family, sisters
and so on, came to have a look at me in my uncle's house. It was the
week before my exam. I sat there quietly, I had to, with my sari
covering my head and pulled down over my forehead, while they
looked at me and talked to my uncle. I felt so nervous,
embarrassed and ashamed to be just an exhibit to be chosen or
rejected. I had no dignity. I had been robbed of that.

No man has to suffer such situations. They asked me a few
questions – what do you study etc. Then my aunt asked me to
fetch them something to eat. The reason I was asked to do this was
that this would give them a chance to see me walking. While I had
been sitting with the ladies, the men had been sitting on the other
side of the room and something which I overheard them saying
made me very worried. All that night I could not sleep from
worry. My husband's cousin had told my uncle that my husband

was a very hot-tempered man. My *Chacha* (uncle) had not taken it seriously, saying only, 'Well, our girl is very good-tempered and cool'. That conversation kept coming into my mind.

Anyway, soon the whole thing came through. My husband sent a declaration through the Pakistan High Commission. It was his consent to a proxy marriage. The *Kazi* (marriage registrar) came and took my signature and that was it. I was married under Islamic law. There was a big reception. At such receptions the usual custom is for the husband's family to bring presents but they didn't – they brought nothing at all. It was clear that they were stingy, because they were certainly not short of money, being business people with both a chemist's shop and a jute business.

After my exam was over I went back to the village. After that, partly because of the hostilities between Pakistan and Bangladesh, and partly because of harassment from British Immigration officers, it took me seven months to get to Britain. At the British High Commission in Dacca the officials always treat people with rudeness and lack of consideration. As far as I was concerned, they simply would not recognize my marriage. I would come with my younger brother from my village thirty miles away, a dangerous and exhausting journey in a small boat, wearing a large *Burkha* (because at that time any woman who showed her face was in real danger of being raped by Pakistani soldiers) and when I reached the High Commission I would be put off and told to come again for another appointment. When I pointed out the terrible journey, the danger involved, the answer would be, 'That is your problem. It is nothing to do with us.' I would say 'But aren't you human beings, can't you see the way you are forcing me to risk my life!' Their stony attitude never changed.

When I finally got permission to enter it was not as a wife but as a fiancée. They simply would not accept that I was married. My brother, who was still in England bought my ticket and it was he who gave me all the instructions about where to go. He was also my sponsor in Britain. My husband never wrote anything at all about my coming to Britain. He often wrote letters to me, but never did he mention anything either about my ticket, or about what I should do to get to Britain, or even about what our life would be like afterwards. He wrote instead about how he loved me most romantically. He lifted stanzas out of poems, say by Rabindranath, about 'you unknown one', or 'you unseen one' or 'woman in the picture', or something like that. I knew even then that it was all a charade. Once the girls in my class at Dacca University got together and wrote a letter to him saying 'We are Babli's classmates, after our exam we want to go out and celebrate in a restaurant so please send us some money'. He never even replied or mentioned the letter to me. Then my friends realised what an unsociable and humourless person he must be.

While I was running around going to Immigration and things in Dacca he never gave me any support. He told my brother that he wouldn't buy the ticket. Meanwhile, the people in the village were wondering what kind of marriage my brother had arranged, because nearly eight months had passed and my husband had neither come, nor sent any presents, nor made any arrangements for me to go to him.

When I came to Dacca airport for my flight to England, the place was controlled by the Pakistani military. They wouldn't allow anyone from my family to accompany me into the building. I and two other girls were making this journey, the other two were also going as fiancées, one to marry a man in Canada and the other to a man in London. My mother asked us to stick together and try to find seats near each other. But inside the airport the Pakistani soldiers started harassing us. First they wanted police verification, then they found many other excuses to try and stop us boarding our plane. They opened our suitcases and scattered our clothing around. Luckily at that point I saw a Pakistani friend of mine from college who was working at the airport. She helped us through the various barriers. Without her, I don't know what would have happened to us. So often, girls going to husbands and fiancés had entered the airport and then never been heard of again, raped and killed by Pakistani soldiers. In these cases, it was only when relations wrote to ask why the bride hadn't arrived that people would guess what had happened.

The plane we boarded was full of soldiers, who having been wounded by Bengalis, were returning to Pakistan. We asked to be seated next to each other but the air hostess arranged for each of us to be placed by a wounded soldier. We cried throughout the journey – to leave home and in such circumstances! The Pakistani men just sat stony faced beside us. In Karachi, we had to change planes and there their relations flooded the airport, crying in their turn for their wounded heroes.

The journey from Karachi was uneventful. But when I reached London, at the airport, it was a shock to meet my husband. The picture he had sent me of himself must have been taken ten years earlier; since then he had aged tremendously. He was a man of about forty, twenty years older than me. I remember he shook hands with me at the airport. So many strange feelings filled me; I could say nothing. My brother and his wife and child had come to the airport too. Later that day, my brother, who by then had realised that the whole thing had been a disaster, asked me if I wanted to go through with the registry office marriage in Britain or not. If I chose not to marry, Immigration rules would have forced me to return almost immediately to Pakistan. After all I had gone through to get into Britain, I couldn't face that. Rather than try to return and face almost certain death at the hands of Pakistani soldiers, I decided to stay on in England. That was the position I was in so I chose to marry.

The first question my husband asked me when we got home was how much jewellery I had. The house at Noushindi had been looted twice, once by robbers and once by the Pakistani military, so I had no jewellery. Even my mother's old jewellery had been taken. On learning that, my husband said, 'Well in that case you will have to do what women in this country do, you will have to pay by working for a wage'. My passport did not allow me to get a job for three months but I looked for one to start after that period. I had, after all, an M.Sc from Dacca. I went to many, many interviews but everywhere I was rejected. One agency told me that M.As and M.Scs like mine had no value, people with these qualifications were considered no good even for manual jobs. All these experiences of mine drove my husband into a fury because he realised that he would have to maintain me. Of course he had plenty of money both in Dacca and here but he kept telling me what a lot of trouble he had paying for my food.

I lived with him for a few months but we were never together. I always slept in my own bed. All through this period there were insults not only about money but over my appearance – that I walked thumping along like a duck, that I was ugly, and over the fact that my father was dead. He told me that a girl who lost her father must always bear the guilt for it, she must be meek, submissive and never face the world. He would also taunt me with my education – 'you have an M.Sc but you have never seen a bathroom geyser and you can't cross roads properly'. He never took into account that in Dacca everyday life was so completely different. He would go on about his own brother's wife in Dacca, how much jewellery and money she had brought into the family, how meek and submissive she was and how hardworking. One

day while cooking in the kitchen, he told me, she had fainted out
of sheer exhaustion. That was what a woman should be like, he
told me, it was the highest a woman could aspire to. She must
work with her face down.

There was no day when I was not insulted, no night which I did
not spend weeping. My sister-in-law, my brother's wife, is
English; in those days it was she who gave me her support. My
brother and my husband became, increasingly, on bad terms. One
day he told my brother, 'In this country you can get a woman for
the price of a cup of tea.' That was the final insult, since, as I told
you, my *Bhabi* (sister-in-law) is English. After that they no longer
spoke to each other.

Everyone could see the agony I was going through. One of my
husband's friends, also a barrister, told me 'Try to get a job and at
the end of two years give him all the money you have saved, then
perhaps he will love you.' I was silent but I wondered if it was
possible, or worth it, to buy love.

Although I spent so much time weeping, I never wrote to my
mother about it all. I thought there was no point because I knew
that she would be terribly hurt. Then one day my mother wrote to
me, 'Every night in my dreams I hear you weeping, tell me what
has happened'. But still I wrote nothing. The agony of my life
went on. My very identity was debased and degraded: I was ugly,
my family were contemptible, my brother was a bad man, my
education useless. Everything about me was wrong. I could never
answer back. I was unable to. It was a new country, a new
environment, I had always been a quiet girl. I was now stunned,
dazed and terrified by this experience. My husband had always
been aggressive and threatening. One day he threatened to
strangle me. After that my brother and sister-in-law said I should
not live with him. I came to live upstairs with them.

By this time the hostilities in Bangladesh were over, Bangladesh
was independent. My mother decided to come to Britain for a
visit. Even at the airport she knew what had happened. She said to
my brother, 'You are my eldest son, I trusted you but what have
you done! It would have been better to throw her in the water than
to marry her to such a man.' My brother said he never knew, never
understood. My mother told me 'What has happened has
happened now. It is better to put it behind you, to study and get a
job and start living again.' So, instead of asking him for a divorce,
I myself filed a divorce. I had to pay costs and everything. You
see, in this country proving cruelty would have been impossibly

difficult in spite of the suffering I went through and the pain my mother suffered. The whole thing has taken me nearly seven years and even now it is not quite complete. Think of what this marriage has done to me, seven years of my life gone and what is there in the future? For my husband these seven years don't matter so much. He said that even when he is fifty he can go back and marry a young girl in Bangladesh, and it is true because he has a house and he has money.

As for working in this country, there is always a doubt in people's mind whether an Asian woman in a sari is capable of doing a job which requires intelligence. So finding a job was a struggle. But at last I have got a job which I like, my work is what I really care for. But apart from that there is nothing in my life. I have no English friends who want to see me after work; with Bengalis making friends is not easy because they want to know all the details of your past, few people care what you are really like. But compared to many women I am lucky; at least I had a brother who cared for me and looked after me. When I think of the Sylheti women I know, I realise how many are in a similar position to what I was, only they have no means of escape.

Slowly I am regaining what I had lost – my human dignity. Reading *Nimaz* helps me. Islam considers men and women equal. It is men who have ruined it with misinterpretation.

Arshad:

Before we came here we lived on the outskirts of Rawalpindi. My husband worked in an ordnance factory about 12 miles away. We spent the first six years of our married life living with his parents but a lot of that time they were ill. After they died, my husband's brother and sisters lived with us for sometime but eventually they all got married and left.

I married when I was twenty. He was my *Khala's* son, in fact, to tell you the truth we arranged it ourselves. Yes, we wanted to marry each other. Our parents didn't want it because my mother and his mother had had a quarrel and for thirteen or fourteen years they had stopped seeing each other. Then his father was posted to our town, (it was a very small town outside Rawalpindi). Sometimes my husband would come to visit us. We would quietly glance at each other or sometimes even secretly talk in very low tones. And from our smiles we could tell the state of each other's hearts. But he could hardly tell me directly that he loved me. As for me I knew from my own heart that I loved him but of course I could only guess at his feelings from the way he behaved. But he is very quiet, has always been very quiet. In the end he told his father 'I want to marry into that family'. After that a letter came to our house for my father with a proposal. My sister tried to hide it from me but I could guess who it was from and what it was about because the same feelings were in me. Slowly you see our feelings had developed.

We have been happy together. Our life together has been a fine life. We never quarrel with each other. It is true, though you are laughing. We never quarrel. He is perhaps more quiet and subdued than I used to or wanted to be. But one cannot have everything in life and anyway we are happy. I am free, to do what I like, go where I like.

In my mother's house, I was always rather independent minded. My mother used to say 'We don't know what kind of husband you'll get or won't get so until you are married you should observe *Purdah*. And now you are getting older people might talk if you don't wear a *Burkha*.' So when I went to school, I used to wear a Burkha on the way. Because you know what it is like there otherwise – people keep following you. If you wear a Burkha at least they don't know your identity. Also, when I was twelve years old, I was tall for my age. When you are young like that, you have a sort of radiance. The place where I lived was only a very small town and people used to gossip, they would say of girls 'She is always lifting her face up and looking at people. She is a girl from such and such a family. What sort of mother has she got who does not make her observe Purdah.' So my mother used to keep me in Purdah and she always told me 'After marriage you can do differently.' But at my wedding she gave me two Burkhas. They were beautifully made *Fashni* Burkhas. The top was like a gown with lovely smocking and the veil was made of the thinnest georgette because I never liked ones with holes for the eyes but ones which showed the face to a certain extent.

After my marriage I wore the Burkha for a few months. My husband wanted me to. But I never liked it, I used to lift it up and go around like that and he used to ask me to lower it. Then one day he said 'Either wear it properly or don't wear it at all,' (laughs) so I said 'All right, I won't wear it at all'. He didn't object. So that was that, his family didn't object, in fact they too became advanced in that respect.

But having said that I must explain that in Pakistan it is not really easy to manage in a town without a Burkha. Even if you wear one people follow you, try to brush against you or pinch you; without a Burkha it is much worse. It is quite horrible that way. Perhaps if the government were stronger these things would change but the government never really does anything about it. Women always have to sit separately in public places, there is no freedom to do what you want. As for work, a few women do work but very few and they are usually teachers or doctors. But then there is so much unemployment even for men.

In England there is more freedom but people are very different from us. For example you are a Hindu and I am a Muslim but when I meet you and talk to you I can feel close to you very quickly and then, as women, there is a real bond between us, but here between women there is rarely any love; there is usually a hardness and dryness. Over there girls are gentler and if they are talkative like me it is easy to be friends. Here I know almost nobody. It is not possible to make a friendship with English people, there is the language problem but apart from that our ways and attitudes are different.

I came here in 1971. We lived in Fulham and I started work in a laundry nearby. It was very hard work folding sheets, standing all day. The wages were low – if I remember correctly it was about £15 before tax. At that time I had just come to Britain. I couldn't understand English, I didn't know the ways and I used to be apprehensive about the weather – I had heard in Pakistan how dreadful the climate was in England, how cold and unpleasant. Because of all this I wanted a job which was right near my home, and by God's grace I got a job which was really near, just about two minutes walk away.

All the workers at this laundry (it was a branch of Sunlight laundry) were English, they never spoke to me. I was shy (because I am like that, all Asian women certainly are not like that, but I am) and I didn't feel that I could speak to them. They never approached me, all day I worked in complete silence. I really wasn't happy there. The heat was extreme, to stand up all day in such extreme heat becomes very fatiguing. There was very little time for lunch, tea-breaks were not known and the pay was different for different people. I got less than the English women. But you see the money was needed.

Now I work at Tate and Lyle and conditions are much better. You see we moved from Fulham and have bought this house in Newham. At Tate and Lyle the work I do is pushing parcels of sugar towards a machine which covers them. We have to stand all the time – eight hours. Still, now I am more used to it. From quarter to eight to four, those are the working hours. After every hour there is ten minutes for rest or as a toilet break. All the employees I work with are women, the only men are fitters and engineers. For a long time I was the only Asian woman. I can speak English now but I still find it impossible to really talk to English women. In any case the machines are so noisy that one can't hear anyone clearly and the work goes on at a terrific pace so it is not easy.

A few months back I had a bad experience at work. I had been allocated to a new machine; you see we are moved round every two or three weeks and one morning I was allocated to a new machine. The machines are quite big with a large conveyer belt, one person has to sit in the centre, the idea is to check the cleanliness of the sugar. That day I had to sit in the middle. But soon after I went in, another woman on the machine – quite an elderly woman – started saying 'Smelly! Smelly! Smelly!' I couldn't hear her properly because the machine was very loud like a railway engine in India or Pakistan, so I went up to her to ask what the matter was. Then she began to push and poke at me; as you know, I am a very shy person so I just went back to my place quietly. After a few minutes she started shouting again 'Smelly! Smelly! Smelly!' I know that an English girl would have taken a packet of sugar and thrown it at her in answer to her taunts but I became paralysed. Then she went and got a spray of an air freshner and started spraying it at me. All the other women on the machine – about eight of them – joined her in following me and mocking me. I don't know what happened to my brain, I felt completely stunned and shattered as though I was going mad. I couldn't move or think. Not all women are alike; for me this bullying was utterly shattering. By eleven thirty I was so upset that I thought I would tell the forelady. I went upstairs to find her but she wasn't in. So I had to come down again and face it till 12.30. During lunch one of the ladies from another machine came up to me she said 'What is the matter with you, Mrs X are you sick? You don't look well.' I told her what had happened and she urged me to tell the forelady. That is what I did, our forelady is good, she said she would sort it out. But after the whole thing I felt so bad, I had to go to the doctor. I was off work for three days. When I went back the forelady came and told me that she had given the old racist woman a good telling-off and she had cried.

Since then I have never been allocated with these women and the forelady had asked me a few times whether things are OK.

These white ladies, and there are a lot of them, some working at Tate and Lyle for 20-25 years, they have always taunted us few Asians, that is the reason I don't like to talk to them. Also when they talk to each other they quarrel so loudly and swear so much it is not pleasant. Among us, as you know, we don't like to swear, we believe in mutual respect. Their manners and temperament are different. That is why I praise Gina (a mutual friend) because she has never used swear words. She is English too after all.

I try to teach my children these ways of ours – I think their future could be good and happy here if we are allowed to stay in peace. As for mixed marriages, I don't think that is possible because the English way of life is so different . . . for example, the way we bring up our daughters is different. From the age of ten or so we start checking them, giving them less freedom, not allowing them to do things just as they like because later on in life they'll have to go to someone else's family where they may not always get what they want . . . For boys it is different, though to tell the truth, I don't like my sons to go out late either. What is your opinion about this?

I think that perhaps the upbringing of children is connected to the arranged marriage system.

Yes it is, Arranged marriage is such an important part of our culture. We don't use force, that is not a part of our culture. It is not as though a boy and girl are tied together without being given a choice or without being consulted. I have been happy in my marriage. My husband, he is just not the sort of man who quarrels. Sometimes if I get a bit irritable he says 'I just don't want to have a row.' Then he puts on some music. Other days, if I am depressed, or if he thinks I am, then he says 'Come now, what is the matter, let's go out and forget about it.' We go for a ride in a bus, the two of us, and feel happy together.

Maya:

I was born in England. My father died when I was eleven. Up till then life had been very comfortable and very easy. When my father died I gradually realised that there had been an English community who had been coming and seeing my father and who had suddenly stopped when he died. He was a very able doctor and he had done well. He had been here during the war. English people related to him very well, I felt they related to him better than they related to my mother. Anyway, after the sympathy notes and so on, we never saw them again and we never got any presents as we used to. Perhaps it was that which first started me thinking about relationships. I became very introverted, I felt I was going through the problems of life with my mother. I became very close to her. Both my brothers were away and I was the only child at home. She used to shout in her sleep. She really must have missed my father a lot and I felt that I went through it all with her.

I then decided that I wanted to work with people. I became very aware of people's minds, people's motives and of the pressure on my mother to go back to India because relatives felt that because she was a widow she shouldn't be independent as a human being. That was the kind of mental torture which she had to face and which she had the courage to fight against. Only because she was in England could she be independent and have a say in the upbringing of her children. She often admitted to me that if we had been in India we would have been brought up entirely by a maternal uncle. I have realised since then that my uncle resented the fact that my mother wasn't under him after my father died. He criticised her a lot; even after she died he said 'If she hadn't been so *Azad* (freedom loving) her children would have related better to the family structure back in India.'

My mother did get on with certain groups of people but she never mixed a lot with Patels here. It is because of their attitudes, and it was true, nine times out of ten, that when they did come close they were always criticising my mother for bringing us up the way she did and giving us too much freedom. I think she wanted to give us freedom. When she didn't give us freedom it was because of the pressure of society and because she was a widow. These problems had not occurred so much when my elder sister was growing up because my father was alive.

My mother had a pension, a medical pension, but we were quite badly off. My father had left some money, but most of that was used for my sister's wedding. My sister married after my father died and in a way I felt that my mother wanted to prove that she could marry my sister off independently of the family in a way my father would have wanted. She was very much a society woman in a funny kind of way, conscious that people were ready to criticise, so she spent a lot of money on the wedding which I think she shouldn't have done. So we got worse and worse off, but all the money which she saved was used for our education. She wanted it all to be used for educational purposes. I became very conscious of hypocrisy and really began to hate parts of Indian society. I could see that she wasn't so vulnerable to this kind of thing, I could see that she was game for it and I wished she wasn't.

When I was about sixteen or seventeen I met a man who was eight years older than I was and I became very emotionally involved with him. It was funny because though I had a very close relationship with my mother I felt I couldn't tell her. She was free about everything but I felt the marriage aspect would be the one thing which would really, kind of – kill her. I was really scared because she had been through such a lot. She wasn't pressurising me towards an arranged marriage but she wanted somebody who was acceptable in the Patel community and who was well educated; there were certain patterns laid out. This person that I had got involved with was from UP [Uttar Pradesh in Northern India]. When I look back on it I wonder how I coped, I couldn't have coped now if I had to but I actually managed to cope by seeing him for two minutes on my way back from school or planning for three or four weeks if I wanted to spend an evening with him, and lying about it and feeling really guilty. When I came back from seeing him I used to keep watching my mother, thinking that she knew about it. The guilt was so bad because I felt that we were so close and yet I couldn't tell her about it.

Q. Did you know definitely that she would disapprove?

She made it clear in her values that she didn't believe in love marriages and that she hadn't had a love marriage and her marriage had been very happy. At that time my sister had had an arranged marriage and she was going through trauma (now she is very happy, of course). She had to spend about four years adjusting to this chap and I felt it was too much. Why should she be forced to? . . . If my mother knew the way I was talking now she would probably start crying because she didn't mean me to go through such unhappiness, she never knew, never realised. This kind of hide-and-seek became a part of my life. The only person that I was able to tell was my brother, elder brother. He was supportive but not supportive enough to be able to tell my mother. Because he also felt that she had been through such a lot, and her health was bad, he felt that if he told her it might really affect her.

Anyway I went through a crisis and decided not to do medicine.

I wanted to do something with people, I was very waffly really. Nobody in my family supported me because it was quite easy for me to do medicine because my father was a doctor and my sister had done medicine and I was doing all these science 'A' levels. Suddenly I felt I couldn't stand society, what goes on in society. I couldn't pinpoint it. I wanted to do something with people. And to me, doing medicine was continuing the path of the family. Looking back on it, that was stupid because I would really have liked to do medicine. But to me then it was just following the footsteps. So I just announced one day that I was going to do different 'A' levels, and I wanted to do sociology. My mother didn't like it but she left me to it. I worked really hard to prove that I hadn't wasted time. I got those 'A' levels in one year and got the first University place I could get. The first major decision that I made was that I wanted to live away from home, I just wanted to get away from there. I felt so claustrophobic I felt I couldn't think – and yet it was a free atmosphere, it wasn't like these other girls who can't go out. It was an emotional and a moral thing, there was so much morally defined in our family. I felt I had to get out.

Q. What was morally defined?

How you should lead your life in terms of middle-class values. How you are going to be really happy and get married and have kids and marry decent people. I felt good heavens, what is all this life about? The worst thing about that was that I was very lonely; there was no other Indian girl in my school; the only Indian girls I spoke to were children of friends of my mother's and I felt I couldn't talk to them about this. The rest of my friends were English but I felt I couldn't talk to English girls about this sort of thing. I felt they wouldn't understand things – like when I had a birthday party and I used to say – 'Don't bring your boyfriends.' They used to do what I asked but nobody could ever understand – neither did I communicate, nor did they ask about why the hell do you have that sort of party at your house. Just before I went to University I had a birthday party, me and my brothers, all of us together. My mother would cook all the food. Boys and girls would be invited, English and Indian, that sort of liberalism was there but somehow there was this kind of moral thing that certain things don't happen. I remember the kind of trauma it could cause – I had a Chinese friend and my brother had an English friend and they got together at this party and they were going off together and I was almost sweating – I thought, where was my mother and what were they doing, were they round the front or the back! Nobody ever said anything – you just realised, because the moral thing was so deeply ingrained. And I remember I invited this boy I was having this relationship with to this party. But I had to pretend I didn't know him very well. Can you see the conflict, liberalism but with these really strong moral values!

I think I must have had a rebellious streak in me. I don't know why my brothers have never reacted in the way I have. I was really pleased about the fact that I was living away from home but in fact I hated it. I was in lodgings with this really funny woman who had hundreds of rules. I had more physical freedom at home but I felt my soul free living away. Everyone at home kept asking me how I was getting on and I'd say 'Oh, it's lovely' but I hated living away from the family because I was used to the warmth, the food being ready and so much to talk about. After one term I couldn't stand it any more, so I told my mother that my landlady doesn't want to rent a room any more so I am coming home. I wanted to live in the Hall of Residence but there wasn't a place, so anyway I came home.

But I was really ratty when I was at home. I was never at home and in some ways I felt guilty because I had come home. I made everybody's life real hell. The following year I got into the Hall of Residence. I think my mother realised what I was going through. She kept pretty stable. When I was at the Hall of Residence she used to expect me to ring up every day. I used to do that. In the middle of everything I used to remember that I had to ring her up. I used to go home at weekends and I felt I was missing out on something, I didn't know what exactly it was. I had never seen all this freedom before and I felt I had to be in with these English things which I couldn't be in with. It was a very difficult adjustment for me. I didn't study as much as I should have done. I started making excuses for not going home, I said I have to do work. If I gave work as an excuse everything was all right.

In my second year I became much more interested in politics, as a socialist and in women's groups. That was when I really began to question my family. I felt for the first time that I was talking and they were listening to me. I could analyse things and that made me feel fantastically free. Between what I was like in my first year and what I was like in my third year there was a real transformation. It affected my relationship with my family, they were very hurt. I was so angry about my upbringing. I used to have long discussions with my mother and she used to get very upset. She used to say 'You don't respect your upbringing' and I said 'No, I don't.' Later on I found out from her friends after she died that she saw a lot of herself in me. And looking at it now, in her younger days she had been in the freedom movement. After that her father told her never to go into politics and she used to tell me 'Whatever you do, don't go into politics.' But she believed in horoscopes and all the *Joshis* had told her that this is the girl who is going into politics eventually and she was scared of it.

Q. Why was she scared about it?

Because she thought that I would not accept the fact that I was a woman and she used to say 'You'll have to accept the fact that you are a woman.' And after that period she used to say 'Perhaps I have given you too much freedom, perhaps if I hadn't, you wouldn't have reacted like this'. But she never had these difficulties with my sister. My sister always enjoyed her role as a woman. Then she started looking for various boys, there were some offers from boys living in Bombay, from well-off families. But with this consciousness I had developed I just couldn't do what I might have been able to do before. You see, my mother *was* politically aware, she was critical of the Patel community and she was also conscious that women were oppressed, but she felt that it was up to women to do what they could within the set up. She used to tell me 'You will be radical by doing little things, I am radical by example, I have proved to people that I can do it,' which she did. But in spite of that, as a woman she was very conservative. She encouraged us all professionally but she still felt that a woman's role was to be a mother and to fit into the social set-up, she felt that you should be able to do both. During that period I had almost accepted the dual life I was leading because at University I was known for being very radical.

During that period my relationship with the boyfriend I told you about became very intense. His mother was not well and his father was putting pressure on him from India. You see, he had a childhood marriage, arranged, but he never lived with this woman. But her family had been pestering him all that time to go back and they had been demanding money. I knew that my mother would never accept all that and his father kept writing 'Tell her mother everything, don't get involved with a girl like that without telling her mother.' And he was brought up to respect parents. He kept saying 'We have got to get married, we've got to do something about it.' I kept saying 'She's not very well but I'll tell her if I can.' And I remember having a sleepless night and the next day I was just sitting by her and she was lying on the bed. She started saying something about 'You must start thinking about marriage.' Then I said 'as a matter of fact . . .' and I just carried on. She just tried to ignore it as though it wasn't really there. She got really upset, her eyes went all red as though she was going to cry and she walked out of the room. Then she just carried on.

We had a meal in the evening; she had obviously been very upset. She created a terrible atmosphere. My brother said to me 'What's happened?' I said 'I've told her.' He said 'Oh God! She's going to be in a mood.' I really wished I hadn't told her. I really felt for my mother so much, I felt she had suffered so much. She had lost her mother when she was born, her father when she was fifteen, her husband when she was forty and I felt – what am I doing now? The funny part is she never told me not to do it. She was hurt and I couldn't take it. She was hurt because I had done this without telling her, and that I wanted to marry someone who was older and non-Gujerati. Actually I didn't even tell her that he had been married before. I felt that if she only got to know him she'd really like him – but no way! I went back to college, I remember being very distressed about it. I told him, I can't face her. I can just sort of marry you and go away. But he kind of really respected my mother and Indian boys do have this feeling about mothers. He said, 'You, knowing you, you won't forget it for the rest of your life and you'll give me hell because you'll feel guilty.' And I think he was right, because the relationship with my mother was such an intense thing, I'd never have forgiven myself. We went through a very bad time in our relationship. We went on holiday and tried to be happy. Then my mother was going to India that December and she wanted me to come with her. I said I would, and I told Ramesh that I was going and he said 'OK I'll go too, maybe in a different environment, if she meets my parents in Delhi it might be better.' Then something happened; I think I had to give in my thesis. I said 'I'll go two weeks later.' He went off to India and he wrote to me that his father was really putting pressure on him that I must really come quickly because he was the eldest and they couldn't get the younger brothers married because of him. He had sorted his previous marriage out by that time by paying a lot of money.

After that I don't know what happened to me. I began to think if I marry him I am going to be a housewife for the rest of my life. Other things began to prey on me. I had become so much more politically involved. I thought 'I am being the biggest hypocrite, I'll end up losing respect for myself.' So in the end I didn't go, I really wanted him but I didn't want all the other things which went with him. In the end he had an arranged marriage to someone. At the same time I didn't want to upset my mother, that was very, very strong. I don't know which relationship was stronger. But through it all nothing was said and long afterwards she apologised, she said she hadn't realised that I felt so seriously about it, that if she had known she wouldn't have got in my way. But the funny thing was, how did she know she got in my way. She never said 'No don't marry him.' But I went through a very bad phase.

It really affected my relationship with my mother because afterwards I felt that she had – had ruined my life. Because I wanted him you see, I really wanted him. And he was very unhappy to be pushed into an arranged marriage. Now he has settled down. I am now quite friendly with his wife but, at first, when she got to know me she really looked down on me. She said 'You are very cheap. You could have married him. Why didn't you marry him if you had an affair with him? I know what girls in this country are like.' He was still just very fond of me; he was not getting on very well with his wife at the beginning. Meantime my mother died and I felt this horrible feeling that I had not married him just to please her, keep her happy. She had died, he had married and I was just left out. Out of it all had come nothing, it was a complete waste of time. Do you see what I mean? It is so futile, what goes on in Indian families. There is nothing said, but there is so much guilt.

Q. Do you think there is more guilt when there is more freedom?

Yes I think when it is laid down you know what to rebel against. You have some concrete thing to say – she did this or that. But this liberalism only leads to guilt. I could never turn round and say my mother treated me harshly. There was nothing she said she wouldn't allow me to do. It was most strange.

After that relationship I decided I would never get involved in a relationship like that. Also I found relationships with Indian men very suffocating. I felt that Indian men had a stereotype of what educated westernised Asian girls should be and are, they are curious, think you are some sort of freak and, for example, if you were seen in a bar in the University they would come to all sorts of conclusions. They were so insecure and so worked up about why these Indian girls weren't coming and talking to them and performing the role that they ought to be. In fact one Indian chap said 'You are not proper Indian girls are you?' What is a proper Indian? Actually I felt very Indian. There were things that I didn't agree with but I didn't particularly want to go to discos and sleep around the place or to wear miniskirts – those were the things they thought I ought to do if I was westernised. They couldn't make me out. And I found that even our family friends were saying 'Those children, they are very westernised.' When I took them to task I realised that they were talking about the fact that you speak good English and that your manners can be English, that you get on with English people. For East Africans it was this that was westernised, not going to discos and so on, because you did that with other Asians. So there is a racism on both sides. I felt that, being a woman, I was getting it most of all.

I decided that I wanted to work on a thesis about Asian women. I decided to work at this biscuit factory. That was my six months sandwich. I was staying at home at that time, though I never was at home. My mother was terrified of the place. She never spoke about it. She almost seemed to be ashamed of what I was doing. I could feel it but I didn't bother. She obviously didn't like me working in a factory. I used to bring free biscuits home but she refused to eat them. She was ashamed of telling other people. I got friendly with a shop steward at the factory, he used to talk about the feudal oppression of women but I found that he used to treat me in a fatherly sort of way 'You don't really know, and women get used . . .'

I used to work with other Indian women. There were white, supervisors and their attitude to Indian women was so superior, they really treated them like they were daft. The race thing hit me. I thought of the way Asian women were treated in the factory. Till then it hadn't hit me how racist Britain was because I had been so sheltered from it. Everything was fine for me and I had English friends. In the factory I really was able to identify with these Asian women and I met girls for the first time who were talking about being forced into arranged marriages. You see, they were girls together talking about these things. I had never known that before. Till then I had mainly English friends and now I have mainly Indian friends, so I realise that my identity is changing. I felt there had been something, some understanding lacking in my relationships with English people . . . As the racial thing came up, the more I had these experiences, the more I felt Indian. Like when I was looking for a room, trying to live where I was working. It was pouring with rain. I had read this advert in the paper, rung up and asked if there was a room. I went there and he never opened the door. I looked through the window and he was in the house. I went and telephoned and he had taken the phone off the hook. I was so angry I was thumping on the door and he wouldn't open it. In a middle-class environment I had never encountered this . . . At the same time I was seen by Indian men as having a chip on my shoulder because I was interested in the problems of Asian women. There was a lot of antagonism . . .

I have an emotional draw towards India. This year I went for the first time without any family member. I felt very free. At the airport, suddenly you see the brown faces, and, it was funny, suddenly I felt warmed, really warmed by it all. Suddenly I felt I belonged and then I realised how conditioned I was to feeling that I didn't belong with the people I was with. And all of a sudden I could see that I did belong. To me this is fundamental to what racism is. I remember when I came back I was talking to a middle-class Indian woman about this and she said 'You've just got a chip on your shoulder.' It is not that, it is a feeling that the environment gives you. India, I found really comforting, really wonderful. I got to know a lot of Indian men while I was there and I had one or two offers of marriage. I found these Indians really nice, really good looking, good company but somehow I couldn't see my life with men brought up like that. I had gone through so many experiences and I felt somehow that they were very immature. I think that living in this country one is exposed to a lot more experiences. I felt I had lived in different world, they had different expectations. I was a bit depressed because basically I think I would have liked to marry an Indian man in India, more than an Indian man here. But I have decided that I am going to live the rest of my life in India. But there is a sort of gap there because I don't know how I am going to lead my personal life.

I had got to know a chap here, what shall I call him – Ameesh. I really liked him a lot but he was living with his family. He felt that he couldn't leave them and that individualism shouldn't destroy family life. I could see his point quite clearly but I could also see that my upbringing just would not allow me to live in a group. It seems almost a selfish thing to say and I had always thought yes, in theory I could. I don't find it difficult to relate to people in a group. But when I came to think of how fond I was of him and how I would have to share him with all these people, and that our relationship would be least important – because in Patel families there is so little importance given to the relationship of a married couple . . . He sees my attitude as Western individualism; he says 'You used to argue about the break-up of the family and yet you yourself would be breaking up this family.' I agree with him, and I know that he wouldn't push me towards a female role, but this group, the family, would pull me into a stereotype female role and then again I would feel guilty. I felt also that if I invited English people home, for example, there would be a kind of awkwardness. I felt that if I looked back at it thirty years from now I would regret it. I feel I could carry on this relationship and I don't want to marry. But you know what Indian society is. There is pressure from his family, so I don't know exactly what I am going to do. But I know that I am going back to India. Whereas previously I felt a conflict, I don't now. I feel that all these experiences have made me understand things better. It is just that in all this, where do I fit in?

Tasneem:

I am supposed to be a *Shia*. *Shiaism* is a sect of Islam which does not accept Omar as Khalif. Shias consider that Ali, the son-in-law of Mohammed, became their first Khalif. They are very orthodox and have a religious day peculiar to them. It is *Moharrum*, the anniversary of the death of Hussain, the grandson of Mohammed. At Moharrum people beat their breasts and cry. Moharrum is very important for the women, especially because you go to the mosque, you listen to the lectures and then you really cry. Whatever has been boiling within you, you just cry it out. In Shiaism the women go to the mosque not only for prayers but for these lectures. The lectures are held not only to commemorate births and deaths of religious leaders but also regularly on Thursday evenings and sometimes on other days. If it is a lecture to commemorate somebody's death then a crying session takes place. The men cry too but the women cry much more. Among *Sunnis* women go just for prayers but they don't usually go for lectures. So in that sense Shia women are better off, though in a lot of other ways they are more backward than *Sunni* women.

In Zanzibar, where I was born, there was a big Shia community, at least four thousand people. Usually the men gave the lectures and the women had to listen and there were no questions afterwards. My grandmother came from a town in East Africa. There they used to have lectures at the main mosque and they did not have *Mehfils* as at Zanzibar. She was a talented woman who did a lot of religious studying herself. She used to write articles and religious poetry and a lot of her work was on the rights of women in Islam. Often she did not agree with the men at the mosque. But she couldn't challenge them directly, so she challenged them through articles. She wrote these articles under a pen name and they appeared in various journals, some of which were published in India but distributed in East Africa. There came a time when she and some other women got fed up with the whole situation and with the help of their husbands and some other men they arranged for a place where women could give lectures to women. This was in the 1930s and 40s. Some of the men were enlightened and understood the law but at that time it was quite a revolutionary thing for women to do. Now it is more or less accepted. My grandmother, she was my maternal grandmother, is now dead.

My family lived in Zanzibar. My mother was the only daughter-in-law and my grandfather was a big oppressor, but he loved my mother a lot, so sometimes he bypassed my grandmother and allowed my mother to make decisions. But I lost both my grandparents when I was very young so I was really brought up in a nuclear family. My aunties had been married out. Then one of them was divorced and she came back, and another was a widow and she came back. The one who was divorced had to obey my mother. She didn't have any children and she was a divorcée and she more or less went crackers. And it was definitely because of the oppressive environment she was in. My other aunty, who was a widow, had a daughter. She too came back, because that was the custom – you have to live with your brother if your husband dies. She made no decisions, she had to follow everything that was done in the house. They were, had been made into, useless women. My aunty's decisions about her daughter had to be made by my father. Because she wasn't educated she couldn't stand on her own two feet. She had inherited a lot of money from my grandfather but my father did all the outside work for that, like getting the interest from the land and so on. So she had the money but she was made to feel that she was incapable of creating her own unit to do whatever she wanted. Also it would have been unheard of in that society. It would have meant shame for the family.

I was the second daughter of the family but the sixth child. My sister was the eldest. Unfortunately she had to go through with the whole thing, leaving school at a young age, getting married at the age of fourteen and all that. And I am saying this because I used her experiences later. Then came my four brothers and that meant a lot of investment in education, sending them abroad for studies – and then I came.

I was sent to a Convent school. It was a co-ed school, but because of the segregation of roles and the business of *Izzat* and *Khandan* and all that, I wasn't supposed even to look at the boys, let alone say hello to them. Any time I went out with my mother or family and I saw my classmates I had to ignore them. I was torn between on the one hand affecting my *Khandan* and on the other my classmates in school calling me a snob.

Q. How did the Khandan come into it?

Because the whole Khandan would be affected if I was seen talking to a boy . . . I don't know what my father's concept of education is, he probably sees it as a compartment. But he did not realise that in school I would be absorbing a lot of alien values. He thought I'd just go to school, become clever – that's it. This created a lot of conflict. For example, I was never allowed to go to parties, I knew I'd have to accept that because I knew there was no chance of my arguing it out. I had to say 'Right, I can't go.' Picnics, occasionally I was allowed to go to them. But because of the sort of family I was from I was able to get a lot of social life. I used to go on outings and holidays, but always with the family, not with children of my own age. I had a very good relationship with my classmates but I couldn't spend any time with them socially and that hurt. When they made sports compulsory in school, I thought I really could argue about that. My mother was very much against it, she said I was healthy and I was getting plenty of exercise. They didn't want me to take part in sports because of the dress and because it would be in an open place where men would see me.

When I went out with my family we went to beaches, secluded beaches where we could swim and play without outsiders seeing us. It was like *Purdah*. We hardly went shopping except by car. It was really like *Purdah*. They were very well off and in a way that was the unfortunate thing. They were able to give me things which they called freedom. They'd say I could go swimming, for example. In the end I was able to go to sports only on condition that my brother took me there and brought me home. It was very embarrassing. I felt I was special. It gave you a terrible feeling of elitism. Everything was a battle, everything needed reasoning and because of that you found that at the age of eight or nine you were no longer a child. You couldn't be a carefree child.

However, I became very close to my father, maybe because my brothers were away. I was able to discuss a lot of things with my father. He was a very reasonable man, he believed strongly in education and was a very very orthodox Muslim. So I was able to use Islam to get my way. When I reached puberty there was a lot of pressure on me to wear a *Burkha*. In fact the Burkha was already bought. In that period my maternal grandmother came to Zanzibar and I was able to use her to a certain extent in my arguments against Purdah. She did not think I should wear Burkha. She had an orthodox way of looking at it. She said 'If you wear it now and you marry a modern husband and he makes you take it off, then it is bad.' So I managed to get rid of that.

When I reached the age of fifteen I wanted to do as my brothers did and go abroad for my studies. But my parents were already thinking that I should learn more domestic skills, that I should go to classes to learn how to sew and knit so that I could become a good housewife. A lot of proposals of marriage started coming, not because of my qualities but because of the status which my family had in the community.

My father didn't want me to go abroad. He said 'Look why do you want to go, you can get married and your husband can look after you.' I said 'I agree with you that my husband will look after me (I didn't agree but I had to use his own arguments). But supposing after I get married I am divorced, like you own sister, or become a widow, like your own sister, would my brothers take me in? They are abroad taking their education, I don't know what they would be like when they come back. They may not be like you. Not only that, maybe I won't get along with their wives. Thank goodness your sisters are getting on well with my mother! But if I have some sort of education I'll have a choice later, and I can stay with one of my brothers when I am in London, I won't have to live on my own. When I come back I don't have to work because I know that may not be accepted, but I'll have the piece of paper which I can use later if I need to.' My father felt bad and very guilty because he could see how his own sisters felt. So he said 'As far as I am concerned it is all right, provided your mother agrees.'

I am saying this as though it was only two or three days, but it took a long time, a whole year of discussion. Eventually my mother was consulted. She would spend time crying because she didn't want me to go away and I would sit and talk with her. It was really painful. She thought that I shouln't go away, I should get married. She was afraid; she doesn't like Europeans very much. She says they are like animals and I'll become like an animal. They don't have culture and so on. She really thinks that they are uncultured people.

My brothers were consulted. Two of them were completely against. Two were for it, they said they would look after me. And it so happened that one of the ones who was for it was very religious himself, so that really carried it. In fact when he heard that my father was thinking about it (my brothers used to send tapes, they used to send them to my mother, my mother would sit down and listen and cry) he started talking in these tapes about what would happen once I got here, how I would live with his landlady and how he would take care of me. So he went out of his way to eliminate any fears my parents might have had. In the end I was allowed to come and they knew that my college, Bedford College, was only for girls! At that time I thought I'd probably go back and get married and work but I had no clear idea. I never, for example, thought that I would have any relationship with men other than Shia men. A lot of things came through evolution!

I came over and I lived with the couple my brother had lived with. It was in Woolwich. At home I had met the colonials, the elite. Here again the British Council with Rolls-Royces had arranged everything so I was naive enough to think that the British people were homogeneous, all speaking the same sort of language. I was surprised I couldn't understand my landlady who was a cockney. When I spoke to my landlady I would look down, I would never look her in the eye. She had small children; it really reached a crisis and I might have been thrown out of the house. Then she asked me why?

We discussed it all and I told her that in my culture we don't look anyone, and particularly an older person, in the eye. She told me 'In our culture if you don't look into somebody's eyes that means you are telling a lie. It is a bad example for my children.' I thanked her for telling me and from then on I tried to look into her eyes. Her other complaint was that I was very rude, I didn't say thank you, didn't say please. So I explained the whole thing, I explained to her that in my culture it should be a pleasure for her

that I don't say thank you because I have accepted her household
as my home. If I was living there as a guest then I would say thank
you and please. It was rude in my culture for friends of mine who
came to my home to say thank you and please to my parents. My
parents would really be upset if my friends said to my mother, for
example 'Thank you very much, lovely food.' They were difficult
concepts to explain to my landlady, but I tried. But I told her that
I would say thank you and please as often as I could because,
obviously, my culture does not apply in this country.

I had come from Zanzibar, a very pluralistic society. In the
school we went to we had Chinese, Japanese, black Africans,
Arabs, Asians, people of different colours and religions, and I
never thought colour was important. Here, after the Pakistani
mass migration of the early 1960s, the papers and the television
were laden with racism. It was very upsetting. I reached the point
when I used to go on the bus and look at who sat beside me.

I did my 'A' levels, and a lot of boys tried to talk to me and to
ask me out. At the beginning I used to be frightened. I used to say
'No! No!, of course not' I'd be rude to them because I thought that
they had the cheek to ask me out with them – these boys, some
black, some white, not even Asians. I thought that was a cheek. At
that time, being a Muslim I didn't drink, didn't eat pork, tried to
read the Koran and say my prayers as much as I could. I belonged
to the Shia International Union formed by East African students.
We used to meet and have religious gatherings or sometimes
outings.

But gradually as I lived in this country, I started thinking about
things and I found myself changing. I fell in love with an English
boy, Steve. At that time I knew that the relationship wouldn't last
long. In that sense it was like a business, I thought I would go back
and it was temporary. It was like that right from the start. It was
my first relationship with a man outside my home. I thought it
was someone to go out with, nice company, we had lots of
discussions, mainly about politics. We were kind of growing up
together. We discussed Marxism and feminism, those were the
two main things.

The revolution in Zanzibar took place in 1964. My parents had
to leave because they were landowners. They decided to go to a
Muslim country and decided on Pakistan so I was more or less a
refugee left in this country. Probably after that I felt more free,
although I didn't accept living here as permanent because I knew I
would have to go home. But it was funny because I knew that the

immediate community I knew in Zanzibar would have changed and I wouldn't have to go back to them, and so everything changed.

But all through I thought things out very carefully because I didn't want to feel guilty. Even if I went out with this man, we never slept with each other. At that time virginity was very important. To go out with him was a revolution in itself; to sleep with him – I never even thought I would. I still was a very religious Muslim and I didn't drink. I did my degree and I got another scholarship to do some work at LSE. By this time I had become strongly socialist. Zanzibar had joined Tanganyika and become Tanzania and I was very idealistic about socialism. I was reading, writing and thinking a lot about it and I hoped I would be able to serve in Tanzania.

When I left Zanzibar I had a British protected passport which does not mean anything. It expired while I was a student. Zanzibaris abroad are not allowed to hold any passport. This was an embarrassment for the Tanzanian High Commission, because I was a Tanzanian but also a Zanzibari and therefore not allowed to hold a passport. Also it was illegal to live in a foreign country without a passport. I was a foreigner here with an expired passport. So they gave me a Tanzanian passport but at the end of it they put a stamp – 'For any renewals, consult Zanzibar.' The Union between Zanzibar and Tanganyika is a ridiculous union in the sense that each part has its own laws. As a Tanzanian born in Zanzibar I cannot work on mainland Tanzania without getting immigration clearance from Zanzibar. But when I got my passport (unlike, say, my brothers who were offered only one-way passports to Zanzibar) I was really pleased, and that encouraged me to go back.

At that time I was really close to Steve but I had made the decision, so we split. He obviously couldn't come with me and I wanted to go. That was in 1971. But I had great difficulty in getting a job. Finally the Ministry of Rural Development got special clearance for me to work. I was involved in the dissemination of the ideology. My job was development of curricula within the ideology. It was a very interesting job. But I was very unhappy there because all the time I was conscious that I was a Zanzibari and could be victimised, because, being still very idealistic, I was saying a lot of things which people felt I shouldn't be saying. Also I was able to talk with men but I couldn't have any relationship with them because they had wives. The wives of these intellectuals used to stay at home. So on the one hand I wanted to talk to them, on the other I felt that if I did I would be accused of trying to steal them. I felt out of place. It was very, very oppressive. There was also the question of my passport, it was near expiry and I knew that it wouldn't be renewed by the Zanzibari authorities. So I left almost overnight. I had been there about eight months. I came back here.

Surjeet:

I came to Britain when I was three years old and lived in the central part of X—— at the time. It was an area with a lot of other Sikh families. My father had been here two or three years before he had sent for my mother. We were from a village in Punjab, a village – mud huts, the lot. We had land and we still have land, land is the most important thing there and my parents have often been back to keep an eye on it. We had moved into the village during the partition troubles. Before that we had been in some obscure place in Pakistan. But we had quite settled down in the village.

When my parents first came to X—— they shared a house with my aunt and uncle, and then they moved out and became lodgers somewhere quite close by, and then eventually we managed to buy our own house. We bought our house in the poorer part of X—— and stayed there till I was about ten years old, and then my dad had put down for a council house and we got it and I think that was the main break. Before that we had been stuck in the middle of a lot of Indian families and we were a very traditional Indian family, I suppose. We had relatives dotted around, not immediate relations but uncles and aunts of uncles of aunts. Then when we moved to the outskirts of X—— we were the only Indian family, with all English families around. When I went to school I was the only Indian girl.

Because I was the only Indian girl – later there were a few others – I was very aware of what I was and I didn't want people to think I was different. I didn't want to tell them what went on at home – for example, about the food we ate. I would never talk to my friends in Punjabi or anything like that. It remained like that all the way through. I wanted to be with English friends and to be like them.

My mother started working when I was about fourteen; then it had become trendy for women to start working. Before then, no Sikh women worked at all. A few of them started working in a local factory where there were only Indian women, so the husbands thought 'well, money coming in and they are only working across the road and we know there are no men working there.' My mum worked in a bakery, there were only women working there, almost all of them Indian, and only one man – the boss.

When I was about fifteen, the sixth form looming, I was not interested in staying on at school at all. We were quite a traditional family. I didn't know what I should do next. At home I wore *Salwar*. I used to hate it. I daren't go out in case my friends saw me. So what I used to do, I remember, I used to get it so dirty that I had to take it off and put my dress on. But at school we had uniform and I could say to my parents 'I have got to wear uniform.' They accepted it. Then *Pyamas* (flared loose trousers) came into fashion. I didn't mind them so much but I still only wore them round the house. I was allowed to go to certain school functions but not in the evening. I didn't really go out much at all. My brothers and sisters were younger than me so I used to end up looking after them.

But things began to change when I was in the sixth form. My father gave me the choice. He told me – 'Either you stay on and get your qualifications or you stay at home and do the housework.' Because at that time girls didn't go out to work. Mums had just been allowed to, but girls hadn't. So I stayed on in the sixth form. Then I decided that I wanted to be a teacher. With Indian families the prestige is either in teaching or medicine, nursing, well, not so much. I definitely didn't want to go into medicine so I decided on teaching.

I wanted at that time to find out what the outside world was like. Being shut at home and seeing your friends going out and being able to wear any clothes they liked made me feel very restless. I wanted to get out, to go to a college away from home, but I didn't know how to set about telling my parents I wished to do that. I made lots of reasons up. The main one was that there was another Indian teacher, a young girl who was already at college in London somewhere, so I said to my parents – 'look, she is in London, she hasn't grown bad or anything like that.' And I was very thankful because my parents had enough trust in me to know that I wouldn't do anything bad! I also said I couldn't study at home because of my younger brothers and sisters, who were going through a very noisy stage. They agreed. I managed to get into a college away from home.

And after that, I changed. I was away from home, within

reason I was free. The thing I liked most of all was English music and dancing. While I was at school there was one disco I went to, just one. You can imagine, I was eighteen. In fact I think that was the reason I chose the college I did, because in the prospectus I saw this small photograph of a dance. It sounds silly now, but that sort of thing appealed to me. I went to the college discos and at the college I made a few close friends. I tried drink but I hated it. But when I went home I would go back to what I used to be, because I didn't want my parents to think that now I was at college, look what I was doing.

The first main break I made was in clothes, because in college you just wore jeans and tops; at home I was allowed to wear trousers but only with something long, something which came below the bottom. Gradually I began to wear my college clothes at home. At first they weren't too keen, but the fashions were changing, and some other girls had started to wear them as well. Also because I was training to be a teacher and you are allowed a certain something if your daughter is training to be a teacher and you can tell other friends and relatives it is because she is a teacher she's got to wear those clothes.

I was at college for three years. In the first year I didn't want to go back at all but by the third year I didn't really want to live on my own. I thought it might be complicated and I am close to my parents and I would have missed them. I ended up going back home, and I think that was probably my mistake.

I got a job in X—— as a teacher. I was there for nearly three years. It was the Christmas before last that they started arranging a marriage. Before that they had received other offers but they were mainly from boys from India, from other villages nearby to ours. But I didn't want to marry a boy from India. Then there were some offers from boys in England. They came to see me, at the house of the person who was arranging it. My mum made sure I dressed in Indian clothes at the time. I ended up wearing *Pyama* and a top and she made me put a *Chunni* on my head, which I never did normally. The boy was very tall and he saw my height, how small I was and that was it. And also because I was dressed in very traditional Indian clothes, I didn't even look like a teacher. Anyway I didn't like him at all either. I had said no, even before he did, so it is not that bad.

There was one other person I had to see. He was a very educated person from the University. He was awful! I mean he was quite a sweet boy but he was very short, plump and had a great big moustache. I took an instant dislike to him and said definitely not. There were a few others that I didn't really see. My parents go for looks as well really, so my mother wasn't too bothered when I refused. She said there are plenty of others. After I rejected this one, who was highly educated, my aunt and uncle, they are very close to our family and they are more traditional, they started saying 'Look, she is not interested in educated people.' And by that time I was getting really fed up. I thought either I could run away, but I couldn't do that to my parents because I love them, or I just had to go along with an arranged marriage. By that time I really couldn't care less. I thought I might as well get it over with now.

It was arranged through my uncle. He knew somebody or other at his factory. He said 'He is not an educated person, but then again you have rejected educated people.' I thought, what is education anyway, so long as the person is good and kind, that's what matters.

This arrangement finally came through; the middleman worked in the same factory as my uncle. They brought his family, him and three other brothers. They sat in the front room and I was called upon to go in the front room. There were two settees at right angles and, of course, you can't really stare at each other. It was so embarrassing, can you imagine a room full of people and you are sitting there? I don't think I had a proper look at all. I didn't sit there very long because I was so nervous. Everybody started saying 'Yes he is very good, don't say No'. My mother was saying 'Yes, he is very good,' and my brothers were saying 'He is very nice' and my father was not there, he had gone to India. I think the rest of them just wanted me away, wanted just to get me arranged away. What could I say? I hadn't talked to him at all. I couldn't say anything.

But I did want to know at least what his background was. I kept asking my brothers to find out what their situation was. And I had heard so many good things from the middleman – and from my uncle – 'They have got a lovely big house, carpets, two front rooms.' I asked them how many there were in the family; they weren't quite sure. The middleman said they'd just got a couple of kids each. So I thought it was not too bad.

I didn't tell anyone at school except one teacher who was a close friend. I told the others we were moving. The preparations started – getting the dowry together. School broke up at Easter. I wasn't keen on dowry at all, I thought it was complete waste. At least one thing I didn't have in my dowry was furniture – most people give three-piece suites, beds, dressing tables. I said they have probably got enough furniture in the house, so we just got the smaller things like radios and tea sets and tape recorders and record players and sewing machines! They expected these things. By this time my father had been summoned from India; he went to see them but by that time it had all been arranged.

Everything got under way. They wanted the registry marriage first of all. They insisted on it. That was the first time I really saw him properly, and Oh! I wasn't happy at all but I went through with it.

I am not quite sure what I felt at the time but you knew that you had to go on, you couldn't just say 'No I am not going to go through with it.' I was in a sort of daze, I just went through the different stages of it all. They wanted me to wear a sari but at the time I was anti-saris, I said 'I can't really walk in them, I have never worn one before.' So I wore a long skirt. We didn't say or have to say anything to each other. Afterwards the photographer was taking pictures in different positions but he didn't say a word. We came back in the same car but I had somebody else with me, someone from my family. He didn't say a word. When we got home there was dinner and everything.

The Indian marriage was the following Sunday in the *Gurdwara*. I wore a long skirt, but it was in Indian style and I had made it myself, with a long *Kamiz*, and it was embroidered with silver thread. I hate bright colours and silver everywhere. I must have looked dreadful. But I had to for a wedding. I had a gold set which I wore, and my hair up in a great big bun and I had an embroidered *Chunni* and a shawl, since you are not supposed to show very much. I went through the marriage the same way, really in a daze. Everything just rushed upon me before I could think. I was so upset I just cried the whole way through. Because I was leaving my parents and all the rest of it. After the marriage and after the dinner and everything the girl goes to the husband's family, and I went. All my family were very upset as well.

When I got there, there were hundreds of people milling around, I had the Chunni over my forehead so I could just about see. They had some sort of ceremony, after which the girl usually stays one night and then comes back home. So I wasn't feeling that bad because I knew that it would be only one day and then I'd be back home. That night I didn't have to stay with him, I stayed with other women (that is the custom). I shared a room with another girl. The next day we went to the *Gurdwara* for another ceremony and then came home. I was dying to get back home. On that first visit to my husband's house my brother had come with me, he stayed the night and everything, that is the custom. By that time I had accepted that I was married, the three wives of the brothers, they seemed OK, friendly enough. I hadn't seen the house properly except the room I was in. Then after a week or so the family came over with the other wives to my parents' place, so the brothers came and their wives came. They were all dressed in lovely saris so I thought they were not that old fashioned. At least they were allowed to wear saris – because wearing saris is considered rather modern for Sikhs. Anyway the ceremony when the brothers and wives and children come is called the *Melni*, they meet the girl's family and they exchange gifts. They stayed, had dinner, and I dressed in a sari and then it was the worst part, leaving my family. That was the worst part for my family as well. It took us about three quarters of an hour to get to the town where they lived.

Well the evening progressed, I knew that that was the night I would have to go into the same room as my husband. Eventually, late in the evening I was summonned. We had the front room because, after all they had said about it being a big house, it wasn't really. What it had originally was a front room and a very large kitchen. What they had done was to extend the kitchen area, so they had a tiny kitchen at the end and the kitchen was a sort of living room. So they had one room spare. That's why they said they had two front rooms – prestige! Two front rooms! Anyway that's why we were given the front room.

A completely strange person – I knew I was expected to sleep in the same bed as him. But surely people have got feelings. All I can say is that I was attacked. As soon as I entered the room I was attacked and I screamed. First I tried fending him off but I was so scared I screamed, I just screamed, called for my mum and dad. The whole house must have heard but nobody came; it seemed that it was going on for hours. Eventually there was a knock on the door. It was one of the wives. I just went to her and clung upon her and I wouldn't let her go. I said 'I can't stay here at all. Please let me sleep in your room.' I was really shaking, I was in such a bad state. She tried to calm me, said don't be silly and everything. By this time I had managed to take her out into the living room. Then the oldest brother came and he said 'Either you get back in there or I am going to tell him to come and get you.' So I went back in. What a start!

Slowly I started finding out what the family was really like.

That night, if I could have got out I would have just run, but they had bolted the door. I don't know where I would have gone but I would have; but I couldn't get out. The following day I just sat in one corner the whole day. Slowly I started finding out about the family. There were the three wives, the eldest one had four kids, the next one had five, and the third who had been married for a couple of years or so had three. They were all aged between two and nine. There were three bedrooms upstairs; one husband and wife and a couple of the youngest kids slept in each of two rooms; in the third room were the mother and all the older kids, the third brother and his wife slept downstairs. The oldest brother ruled everything, everything he said had to be obeyed.

In the next few days I tried to calm myself, I thought what can I do really, but there were a number of small things. I didn't want to cover my hair; I couldn't have my hair loose. I thought that might be dicey, I always had it tied back in a bun. Anything western was frowned upon so I thought I'd give it a bit of time before I got into my trousers and things. But I have never worn Chunni over my head so I just wore it round my neck. Their mother kept asking me to wear it over my head. I thought after a few times she'll stop she'll accept it. Then school started and I couldn't wear *Pyamas* to school so I wore my trousers and tops (throughout all this time it was really bad but I thought I had to stick it because what else could I do.) When they saw my clothes for school they said 'Oh! That won't do! You'll have to wear long tops. If you are wearing trousers you'll have to wear long tops so it does not show anything.' But I had not brought any like that with me, all my things were jumpers to wear with trousers, so I thought, let them get used to it.

After a few days the eldest brother told me to come. Everybody was around, everybody could hear him. He said 'In future you'll have to wear Pyamas and Kamiz to school and I have heard that you don't cover your head though you have been asked to. When you go to school you will wear a scarf over your hair and you'll be taken there every morning by your husband.' I couldn't do anything. The next day I had to wear a long Kamiz over one of my trousers and have a scarf covering my head. Can you imagine – going to school like that? I don't know what the headmaster thought but he guessed that something was wrong. It just wasn't me to have to go around like that. I refused to be taken to school, but every morning before I left the other wives would come and put make-up all over my face – bright red lipstick and things. I hate bright colours and I never wear make-up but they wouldn't listen. I used to rub it all off on the way to school.

After about two weeks I went home for a weekend to my parents' house, and before I went to them I went and saw a friend of mine who had been a friend from college. She is English and she's a teacher. When I told her what had happened to me she asked me to leave immediately and come to her. I really wanted to but I couldn't – they had my passport and I had no money and things, and the most important thing was my job. I couldn't just leave that. Anyway I made up my mind that I had to escape. I thought that half term would be the best time because I could get a transfer to another school after that. I didn't want anybody to get suspicious so I continued just as usual. I didn't tell my parents because I didn't really know how they would react. When I went back I was very nervous. I thought they might notice and get suspicious. It was really difficult. I had to wait nearly four weeks till half term.

Everyday when I went to school I would take something small with me, like some of my clothes or some money, and leave it there so that the day I finally left I wouldn't have to take much with me and they would not get suspicious . . . I had planned to leave on the last day of half term, which was a Friday, so the day before that I took all the things which I had been taking to school with me to the station and put them with the left luggage. That night I really was so worried, so frightened, I really was terrified that they might notice something. Next morning I took a bus to the school as usual, then took a bus to somewhere else and then a taxi to the station. I sat with my head down all the time, I was so scared in case someone, some friend of the family saw me. Till I was in the compartment and till at last the train left the station I wasn't sure that I would make it.

I sent two telegrams, one to my parents saying that I was well but that I couldn't go on with my marriage, and the other to my husband's family just telling them that I wasn't coming back. Later my parents told me that their telegram never reached them till the Monday and when they heard that I was missing they were really frightened. They even thought that these people might have killed me.

I had nowhere to live where I felt safe. I went to various friends in different towns, and in the end, when I had to start teaching again, I stayed for some time in a hostel which is run specially for Asian girls who have run away from home. But after that term was over, I moved right away from the Midlands and got a job. After nearly eight months I decided to go and see my parents. That was wonderful. My father put his arms round me and wept and my mother wept too. They said I should have told them, they would have never made me go back.

Ameena:

I was born in what is now Tanzania. My father was a businessman and our family was very well-off and respected. I have no photographs I can show you of myself but in my youth I used to be very beautiful. At fourteen I was married and it was after that that my sorrows started. My husband was a drunkard and he was also not a healthy man, he suffered from asthma. In Kenya where he had lived his reputation had been so bad that he had not been able to find a wife, but unfortunately my family in Tanzania had not been able to find out his background. We went to live in Nairobi where he had a job as a bus conductor on the Nairobi – Kisumu service. He used to ill-treat me. Once when I was pregnant with my first child he beat me up. At that stage my father said I should give my husband up and come and live with him. But I was pregnant. I did not feel that I could leave my husband. When I told my father this he said that since I had not taken his advice and left my husband I should never complain to him again.

Years went past. I had six children – first three sons, then a daughter and then another two sons. In those days I was young. I had lots of hope that my sons would look after me in my old age. Now I have had more experience, I have learnt not to expect anything from people.

In 1954 my husband died. I became a widow but the community looked after me and my children. The Ismaili Welfare Society gave us a food allowance, made an arrangement with the government for us to pay reduced rents. Also all medical treatment was free in special Ismaili hospitals and school fees for my children were paid by the society. In addition I used to cook and sell food to members of the society . . .

After the troubles in Kenya my two elder sons came to live in Britain. I stayed on in Kenya with my third son but I was not happy, I did not get on with my daughter-in-law and in any case life in Kenya was no good, prices had gone up and we were not treated well because our skin was not the right colour. My elder sons in Britain sent for me and in 1974 I finally came here to live with them. But I only lived with them a few months – after that I left them and now I rely on myself. I am happier that way because one shouldn't and can't depend on anyone. When I came to live with them I did everything I could, I cooked for them, looked after the children, I did all these things with pleasure but none of it was appreciated; and then there were money problems – that perhaps was the main thing.

Now I am happier because I am independent – that's the only way. Those first months in England I used to stay with my eldest son but my second son also used to contribute to help pay for the extra expenses I caused. They did not claim social security because although they knew about it they didn't want it. They wanted to maintain me themselves. Somehow problems began to develop, there was tension between my two sons and it was all caused by my living with them. My relationship with my daughter-in-law became very bad. I could not live freely, I felt very conscious of the food I ate.

Q. Was the trouble mainly with your sons or your daughter-in-law?

Oh, it was with my daughter-in-law because my sons had agreed beforehand to pay for me. When their wives found out, that was when the trouble started. But it is a long story and it hurts too much to think about it. Anyway, when I found that the relationship between the two brothers was getting strained I said I would leave them. They found me a room in Willesden Green and to begin with they each of them gave me £5 a week out of which I had to pay rent and buy my food and everything else. It was very difficult. Then a friend from my community told me about social security and finally I started claiming it. After some months I met an Ismaili woman who owned a house in which she let rooms to women like myself. I decided to move in there. I am nearly sixty but I was the youngest woman in the place. The oldest was a lady in her eighties. She was handicapped and there were others who were deaf or partially sighted; they had all been kicked out by their families or forced to leave. I had a room on the top floor and I was not happy about that because I have a heart condition. Another thing which I didn't like about the place was that the women quarrelled continually. Everyone was constantly prying into everyone else's business. The gossiping was terrible. That, in the end, was why I left. I was lucky to find this room with a family who had been my neighbours and friends for thirty years in Kenya.

I am not one for cinemas or restaurants but I am religious and I like to go to the *Jamat Khana* every morning. Here too there is an Ismaili Welfare Society and volunteers from there come every morning at 4.15 to take me to the mosque; I return at 6.00 am.

Q. What else does the Ismaili Welfare Society do in Britain?

As far as I know they don't have many activities except that they do organise these volunteers to take us to the mosque. But at least there is that. Recently one of the Ismaili leaders went to Canada and according to him things are even worse for old people there. There is a large Ismaili community there (infact it is fashionable nowadays to talk of going to Canada), but there is no Welfare Society and nothing at all for old people. They stay at home all day and if they want to go to the *Jamat Khana* they can't even do that because it is usually miles away and there is no one to take them. Of course I don't know all this for sure but that is what people say when I meet them at the mosque.

Q. In Kenya, was it known for parents to be thrown out by their sons?

It was known (the Ismaili Welfare society looked after such people) but compared to what it is like in our community here it was very rare. There was a lot of moral pressure on sons to treat their parents well . . . Now my advice to parents would be never to live with their sons and daughters-in-law. That is what I have learned through harsh experiences. If I had not lived with them I could at least have maintained some relationship, now there is none at all. They never come to see me and I never visit them. Even if I see them at the mosque at *Id*, they never acknowledge my presence. In our culture we do not like to tell people all our feelings, but in my heart there is so much pain.

One thing I look forward to is my daughter's arrival in Britain. She has a British passport and though she has been delayed I think that soon her application will come through. I always wanted my daughter to have an education, I made her do so many courses, in dressmaking, hairdressing and typing. I thought that if one day she had to earn her living she wouldn't find it difficult. But she fell in love with a very wealthy man and got married to him. Among Ismailis love marriages are common because boys and girls meet in the mosque. Her husband was very good to her and she was young and well off. But he died in an accident and she became a widow. At thirty-three – she was so young and she was a widow with two daughters! My marriage had been so full of sorrow but hers was so happy. Happiness – why is it taken away from us . . .?

When she comes to England maybe she and I could have a future together.

VIII
Reflections

Q. Why did you write this book?

Because I felt that Asian women had so much to tell, I wanted to write a book in which they could express their opinions and feelings. There have been things written about Asian women which show them always as a group who can't speak for themselves. They are just treated as objects – nothing more. That they have any feelings about their own lives or that they can analyse their own lives never comes up. I wanted to show how Asian women are quite capable of speaking for themselves.

Q. Have you stuck to a predetermined plan in writing this book?

I had some ideas beforehand, but when I came to doing the interviews I was really carried away by the strength of personality of some of the women. The things which they told me, and their images, haunted me throughout the period in which I was writing this book.

Q. Do you think your book is based on your own opinions or have you reflected their opinions?

I have tried to reflect their opinions as far as possible, but a book like this needs the writer to identify very strongly because it is a very personal book. In doing that, I have in a way been through a lot of things with the women, and that has made me sensitive to their lives. I haven't been able to avoid giving my own opinions. But a lot of the sections in which I have tried to analyse different set-ups – for example the family or the relationships between husbands and wives – have been suggested to me by the women to whom I spoke. They would say 'This topic really needs discussing.' So it is not usually possible to say which part is mine and which part is other people's.

Q. When you interviewed all these different women, did you always find it easy to identify with them?

I found it easier to identify with some than with others. Whether I identified with someone or not depended on a lot of different factors – the language I interviewed them in for example. I speak Bengali, Hindi and Urdu. Some women used their mother tongue – Urdu or Bengali; Gujerati women had to use their second language, Hindi, because I did not know their mother tongue – and of course some of the younger women spoke in English. It also depended on the scene where the interview was done. With a lot of women, I talked to them in their kitchens while their families were out and perhaps those were some of the best interviews. Many of the women told me 'Nobody has asked me about my life before'. Many of them 'made' me their sister. And quite a lot of them cried because, I think, in general their lives are sad. All these things made me tremendously involved with them. After that, when I translated their interviews into English and tried to bring out their personalities as much as I could, it was really like doing it for a close friend.

But of course there are subjects on which many women have views quite different from mine. For example, I didn't agree with many of the views about arranged marriages or about *Sharam* (Chapter 5). But I had to present those points of view. I tried not to argue with these women to start with, but after I got to know them well I would discuss these things with them and I have used some of these discussions in the book.

Q. Do you feel you could have written this book if you had not been an Asian woman?

Well, I think it would have been very difficult. Because for a start I think that Asian women are very reluctant to talk to white women about their inner feelings. There are two main reasons; first, that they think white women wouldn't understand because they don't come from the same background; and the second reason is that Asian women are aware of living in a very racist society, and this casts a shadow over their relationships with white people unless they know these white people very well. Many Asian women feel that they shouldn't criticise their community or criticise anything that happens in their community to outsiders, and that too is a direct reaction to racism. Occasionally when strikes are reported, for example, you might get a good interview with Asian women, say in *Spare Rib*, done by white feminist reporters. In such cases I think what happens is that there is a common interest, a sort of shared experience which is understood by both sides, so people can talk freely. But if the same Asian women were being interviewed by the same feminists about their family life and feelings, I don't think it would be possible for Asian women to be so frank or so open. And if they were, I am not sure that they would be fully understood.

Q. When you interviewed these women, did you think that some of them were less willing to talk because you were writing a book?

I never interviewed anybody without telling them exactly what it was for, what kind of book I was trying to write and also that I would change their names if they wanted. In many cases they were really keen on this book. It helped me to write this book to know that they wanted me to do it. A good example is a woman I have called Shahida (Chapter 7). She really wanted this book. She felt it was important to make a sort of statement of how women felt, how they saw their lives and the sort of injustices they were suffering.

Q. Now you have written this book, what affects you most about its contents?

Something I feel strongly about is that, although there are so many differences in their life styles, certain factors really unite Asian women. Firstly their oppression – although they come from so many different parts of the Indian sub-continent and have so many different religions, there is no doubt that as women there is a special kind of oppression which they face. The second thing that unites them is racism in Britain, and the third is their exploitation as a class – most of them, even those who were middle-class before, are now working-class. What struck me was that all these three things together affected the outlook of these women and it wasn't possible to separate them. You might think of yourself as just a person, maybe with a husband or parents or children, but when you step out of your door you know that you will be looked at by people as just an Asian woman – a black woman. As for class – immigrants come basically because of jobs, of money; so all the women, even those who don't go out to work, are conscious of their class. They are conscious of their families being working-class. One could put it this way – they may feel that when oppressed as women they are being oppressed as individuals, but racism is an attack on them as a part of their family and community, and these things cannot be separated in the identity of a woman.

Q. What do you think is the next step Asian women could or will take?

That is a difficult question to answer. I don't know if it is clear to anybody; it certainly is not to me. Asian women are living in a changing social environment. Their joint families, where they exist, are breaking up. Also the work situation is changing – more and more Asian women are going out to work. They are getting more conscious of their rights and they have already achieved a tremendous amount on the industrial scene – the Grunwick strike proves that. What is happening in the Asian communities is that family units which faced the pressures of a peasant society now face a capitalist industrial society and quite different types of pressures. As a result family relationships and community relationships and values are changing. Whether this change is going to lead to any kind of liberation for Asian women is hard to tell. It may mean that they will just become westernised, ie. they will go from their kind of oppression to the kind which British women suffer. There is a lot of pressure on them to absorb the commercial values, which are frequently based on the exploitation of women. In some communities Asian women have already fallen under the spell of consumerism. For example, in one part of north London, Gujerati housewives stopped breast feeding their babies because it was considered fashionable to use milk powders. If Asian women just become like the 'ideal', oppressed woman presented in the TV commercials for household goods it would be no liberation at all, but simply a chance lost.

Q. Do you think the women's movement could help Asian women?

I think the predominantly white women's movement would be of very little use to Asian women in their struggles to liberate themselves as women. They can support them in their other struggles, and are sometimes doing so. For example, during the Grunwick strike white feminists have gone out there day after day and helped with the picketing. That is the sort of support they could give to Asian women. On the other hand, if they try to solve Asian women's problems for them in their communities it will make their relationships with Asian women very bad, and achieve nothing. Because it would be patronising interference and would be seen as such.

Q. What specific parts of society prevent Asian women's struggles being acknowledged?

As is the case with women's struggles everywhere, the first barriers which women face, apart from those of any immediate oppressors, are from people who in the eyes of the establishment are supposed to be their helpers and protectors – in this case, for example, statutory authorities whose duty it is to help people but who often don't even treat Asian women like human beings or acknowledge that they have any special problems. Other examples of such official 'protectors' are the male community leaders; these people are almost always utterly oppressive of women. They are often the sort of people who get a thrill out of being respected by the lower ranks of the British community relations set-up. You would never see their wives at any meetings or conferences. The fact that these leaders and their organisations exist, but do nothing, sometimes stifles any attempts by women to organise.

Q. What efforts have Asian women themselves made to organise?

There have been quite a few grassroots efforts, which invariably have faced a lot of antagonism, and some of them haven't lasted very long. But it is still a question of trying methods out. For example, in Wandsworth, Gujerati girls tried to get an anti-dowry campaign going. They wrote a pamphlet on the history of the dowry system and tried a leaflet campaign to get more support, but they didn't really succeed. At the moment I know of two projects which sound very hopeful. The first is an Asian women's centre and refuge which is being organised by a group of radical community workers who are all Asian women. The idea is to provide not just a temporary refuge for battered wives but a centre which would provide the sort of counselling and support which are essential in any struggle. The second is a magazine which was launched in April 1977. It is called *The Oppression of South Asian Women* and it is run by a small group of Asian girls who have grown up in Britain. As a mouthpiece the magazine could be very important. It could be a sort of lifeline for hundreds of girls. Its first issue has been based largely on personal accounts and experiences. If it continues like this it could be a real source of inspiration and ideas for action.

Q. Is there hope that these struggles will succeed?

There is hope, because women are beginning to perceive that there can be a happier future and because they have such spirit and because their anger is growing. How long it will take for a strong movement to emerge is impossible to say. These are the early, early days in a conscious struggle.

Glossary

ALLAH: God (Muslim).

BAHU: Bride or wife or daughter-in-law.

BHABI: Sister-in-law.

BIRADIRI: Brethren or kin.

BRAHMIN: see Caste.

BURKHA: Long veiled garment worn over a woman's other clothes to conceal her face, body and identity from men.

CASTE: Caste has in the past been viewed as a five-tier system which divides Hindu society into the distinct groups — *Brahmin* (priest caste), *Kshatriya* (warrior caste), *Vaishya* (shop-keepers), *Shudra* (artisan and labourer caste) and finally *Achutya* or untouchable ie. outcast. However, this is not a realistic or meaningful definition; caste is better understood in terms of a complex hierarchy made up of thousands of communities, each with a fixed occupation, who socialise and marry only among themselves. Tradition demands that the different castes in any village hierarchy relate to each other only in well-defined terms (ie. usually economic or service relationships). For changes in this pattern see pp. 8 & 9).

CHAPPALS: Indian sandals.

CHUNNI: Long light scarf worn by Punjabi women. For a full description see p. 38.

DHARMA: As noun, religion; as verb, worship.

DHENKI: Device for husking rice. Working the Dhenki is a long and exhausting job almost always done by women. For details see *Jhagrapur — Poor Peasants and Women in a village in Bangladesh* by J. Arens and J. Van Beurden, Third World Publications.

DOWRY: Among Hindus and Sikhs the bride's parents pay a dowry to the bridegroom's parents. Its size depends on the status of the bridegroom and his family (see pp. 114—16 for a discussion of the dowry system among Gujerati Hindus. Among Muslims the bride's parents are not, in theory, expected to pay a dowry but in practice they often have to. In fact Islam recommends that the husband either pays or promises to pay a certain sum of money to the bride as a safeguard in case of divorce.

DUPATTA: see Chunni.

GARARA: Wide flared trousers worn by Punjabi women. See p. 36.

GOBIKI SABJI: Cauliflower curry.

HAJ: Pilgrimage to Mecca, an achievement which gives great prestige to a Muslim.

ID: Muslim festival — Id-Ul-Fatr is at the end of the Ramadan fast, Id-Ul-Haj is to celebrate the pilgrimage to Mecca.

IZZAT: This is a complex word, meaning honour, self respect, pride, male ego. For a much more detailed description see pp. 5 & 104.

JAIN: A religious group with doctrines like those of Buddhism but also many similarities to Hinduism. A significant proportion of Gujeratis in Britain are Jains.

JAMAT KHANA: Among Ismailis this means a Mosque which includes a lecture hall.

JARI: Embroidery in gold or silver thread.

JETWA: Artisan caste.

JOSHI: Astrologer.

KAKI: Paternal aunt.

KAMIZ: Long shirt worn by Punjabi women. See p. 36.

KARMA: Sum of a person's actions in one of his successive states of existence, viewed as deciding his or her fate in the next.

KHALA: Cousin.

KHALIF: Chief disciple of Mohammed.

KHANDAN: Community prestige (also sometimes used to mean class). Polluting one's Khandan is like polluting one's community.

KORAN: Islamic holy book.

KURTA: Long, sometimes waisted, shirt worn by Punjabi women. See p. 36.

MAULVI: A Muslim priest.

MEHFIL: Lecture hall.

NIMAZ: Prayers (Muslim).

PAN: Betel leaf.

PART THREE ACCOMMODATION: Temporary accommodation allocated before someone is rehoused.

PAYAMA: Loose trousers worn by Punjabi women.

PURDAH: Literally this means curtain; it refers to the seclusion of women observed by orthodox Muslims.

ROTI: Chapattis.

SABJI: Vegetables or vegetable curry.

SALWAR: Trousers, tight at the ankle, worn by Punjabi women. See p. 38.

SHARAM: Shame or shyness. See p. 99.

SHIA: A Muslim sect.

SUNNI: A Muslim sect.

VATATEBADA: Savoury potatoes fried in batter.

IMMIGRATION ACTS AND THEIR FUNCTIONING

1962 ACT

Those subject to control: all Commonwealth and colonial citizens.

Conditions for admission for settlement: variable number of Work Vouchers.

Dependants of immigrants: wives and children under 16 admitted freely.

Powers of Immigration Officers: may question at port of entry and refuse if not satisfied.

1968 ACT

Those subject to control: black citizens living in Commonwealth

Conditions for admission for settlement: a limited number of Entry Vouchers issued to heads of families (husbands and fathers).

Dependants of immigrants: entry on head of family's voucher. Wives and children of Commonwealth immigrants must get Entry Certificate by interviews at British Consulate.

Special features: mainly to keep out East African Asians. The UK citizen wives of non-UK citizen husbands have no right to entry vouchers.

1971 ACT

Those subject to control: 'Non-patrial' Commonwealth and colonial citizens and 'non-patrial' British citizens born and living outside Britain. 'Patrials' (Commonwealth citizens of British descent) were freed from control.

Conditions for admission for settlement: UK citizen vouchers *or* work permits for a specific job, valid for one year, maybe issued to alien or Commonwealth citizens.

Dependants of immigrants: wives and children under 18, but they must have an Entry Certificate, which is difficult to get and subject to long delays.

Powers of Immigration Officers: may refuse anyone, including an Entry Certificate holder if 'not satisfied'. Can question and detain anyone suspected of being an illegal immigrant or overstayer, anywhere in the country: usually act with police away from ports.

Special Features: husbands and male fiancés of UK residents may be admitted under a Rule which may be changed at any time by the Home Secretary. Humiliating interrogation of black wives.

	areas	language	religion	dress	dowry system
INDIA	Punjab (rural)	Punjabi; Hindi	Hindu and Sikh	Salwar Kamiz	strong
	Gujerat (mainly rural)	Gujerati; Kutchi	Hindu; Muslim; Jain	sari	very strong except among Jains
PAKISTAN	Punjab (Mirpur, Jhelum) and Azad Kashmir; (mainly rural)	Punjabi; Urdu	Muslim	Salwar Kamiz	fairly strong although not prescribed by Islam
BANGLADESH	Sylhet (rural)	Sylheti (a dialect of Bengali)	Muslim	sari	fairly strong although not prescribed by Islam
	Dacca (urban)	Bengali	Muslim	sari	fairly strong although not prescribed by Islam

Table 2: Asian women in Britain: main groups coming direct from the Indian sub-continent

language	religion	dress	dowry system
Punjabi	Sikh and Hindu	Salwar Kamiz	very strong
	Hindu (Patels)	sari	very strong
Gujerati	Jain	sari	–
	Muslim (Shia, Sunni, Ismaili)	sari and sometimes Salwar Kamiz	fairly strong among certain groups

EAST AFRICA

Table 3: East African Asian women – main groups (all from urban background)

Index

Note to the second edition:

Some of the interviews in this book have been adapted for use in the teaching of English as a second language.

They appear in a booklet <u>Asian Women Speak Out: A Reader,</u> which is now available from the National Extension College, 18 Brooklands Avenue, Cambridge CB2 2HN. Price 80p + 20p post and packing for single copies, bulk copy rates available from the College on request.